For Reference

Not to be taken from this room

ALA Editions purchases fund advocacy, awareness,
and accreditation programs for library professionals worldwide.

LIBRARY SECURITY

Better Communication, Safer Facilities

STEVE ALBRECHT

AN IMPRINT OF THE AMERICAN LIBRARY ASSOCIATION

CHICAGO   2015

Dr. Steve Albrecht is internationally known for his work on workplace violence prevention. He is an experienced author, speaker, trainer, and consultant from San Diego, California. He manages a training and consulting firm specializing in high-risk human resources issues, organizational security concerns, and work culture improvement. His sixteen books include *Tough Training Topics, Service! Service! Service!, Added Value Negotiating, Ticking Bombs: Defusing Violence in the Workplace* (written in 1994 as one of the first books on this subject), and *Fear and Violence on the Job.* He is a retired San Diego Police reserve sergeant who holds a doctorate in business administration, an MA in security management, a BS in psychology, and a BA in English. He is board certified in human resources, security, and employee coaching.

Extensive effort has gone into ensuring the reliability of the information in this book; however, the publisher makes no warranty, express or implied, with respect to the material contained herein.

ISBNs
978-0-8389-1330-7 (paper)
978-0-8389-1354-3 (PDF)
978-0-8389-1355-0 (ePub)
978-0-8389-1356-7 (Kindle)

Library of Congress Cataloging-in-Publication Data
Albrecht, Steve, 1963–
 Library security : better communication, safer facilities / Steve Albrecht.
  pages cm
 Includes bibliographical references and index.
 ISBN 978-0-8389-1330-7 (print : alk. paper) 1. Libraries—Security measures. 2. Library buildings—Safety measures. I. Title.
 Z679.6.A43 2015
 025.8'2—dc23
                            2015005575

Cover design by Alejandra Diaz. Imagery © Shutterstock, Inc.
Text design and composition in the Arno Pro and Gotham Narrow typefaces
by Ryan Scheife / Mayfly Design.

♾ This paper meets the requirements of ANSI/NISO Z39.48–1992 (Permanence of Paper).
Printed in the United States of America

19 18 17 16 15   5 4 3 2 1

To my parents, Eileen Hodes and Karl Albrecht

CONTENTS

Preface ix

Acknowledgments xiii

1   The New Library Workplace: Not So Quiet 1

2   Three Keys to a Safer Library: Security-Aware Staff,
    Creative Customer Service Skills, and Enforced
    Codes of Conduct 13

3   Challenging Patron Behaviors 29

4   Common Types of Challenging Patrons 47

5   Understanding Threats and Getting Help 69

6   Workplace Violence: Awareness, Prevention,
    and Response 83

7   Conducting Your Own Site Security Survey 99

8   Community Partnerships: Law Enforcement,
    Mental Health, and Homeless Services 115

9   Staff Development for a Safer Library: Results,
    Not Just Rules 133

APPENDIX A: Library Security Survey Checklist 141

APPENDIX B: Sample Library Security Suggestions for
Site Survey Reports 147

APPENDIX C: Sample Staff Training Exercises 149

APPENDIX D: Want Less Stress? Try More BREADS 155

APPENDIX E: Resources 159

Index 161

PREFACE

I like libraries now and I loved them as a kid. And I'm a "book guy"; reading and writing (sixteen books so far) have been important parts of my entire life. I was also a cop, and for the past fifteen years, I have taught a program called "The Challenging Patron" for dozens of libraries. If you're like me, you may have thought library work was about books and research and study and information management. I quickly learned that it's really about people. And on some days, it can be about eccentric, idiosyncratic, needy, odd, charming, or kind—as well as challenging—people.

Looking back on a career that includes law enforcement, human resources, security consulting, writing, seminar training, and university classroom teaching, I have found my work in threat assessment to be the most useful for libraries. In 1994, I coauthored the book *Ticking Bombs: Defusing Violence in the Workplace* (Irwin), which was one of the first titles on that subject. Ever since, I have devoted much of my thinking and actions to keeping people safe at work. Despite the book's national attention—even an *Oprah* appearance for my coauthor—my pitch for training services was usually declined. Workplace violence was connected to a theme that still exists today: The phenomenon of armed and angry people coming into offices, factories, malls, churches, restaurants, movie theaters, and government agencies. Statistics bear out that the now-familiar "active shooter" (an odd term of art used mostly by law enforcement and taught to our culture by the news media) still is rare enough to be an anomaly, not something for a business owner or manager to worry about. In April 1999, however, a toggle switch for our national consciousness was thrown at a high school in Jefferson County, Colorado. The school shootings at Columbine High School changed the game for all of us: Cops, security practitioners, human resources (HR) administrators, school district officials, and business owners and operators. Soon after, people were calling me and my "early arriving" colleagues with requests for training and site security assessments of their facilities or to assess the risk posed by a bitter, terminated employee, an employee's domestic violence situation, a troubled student on a K–12 or college campus, or a threatening taxpayer, visitor, vendor, or customer. Conversations with HR directors and managers in public-sector city and county agencies often included concerns about the library. I was surprised. What could possibly go on at the library? Isn't it a place for people to read books and magazines? Who's bothering people at the library?

In 2000, Cheryl Gould and the folks at Infopeople in California asked me to design a program to help library staff members deal with challenging patrons. I soon found myself standing in front of the staffs of public libraries, law libraries, and university libraries in big and small cities, urban environments, and rural locales. Even as a child, I knew the library drew some odd people, and I stayed away from them in the stacks. As a patrol officer with the San Diego Police Department, I had escorted from the library a few obnoxious street people and several dozen drug and alcohol enthusiasts, and I had written up a few theft reports for personal property, books, or videos. Only when I started presenting library workshops, however, did I begin to see the rest of the iceberg.

Some libraries seem to attract the poor and the bewildered, the opportunistic crook and the sneak thief, gang members, abandoned or runaway kids, people who can't control their Axis II disorders or maintain sobriety, the sexual predator who prefers children, or the pornography enthusiast who, for some unknown reason, doesn't have his own computer or access to the Internet. I was discouraged hearing one library worker after another tell me that he or she had been flashed by a guy in an overcoat or asked to help print out color photos of bestiality porn. Younger female staff members complained of being stalked by male library patrons who read their name tags or employee ID badges with their first and last names and job titles and used library computers to get personal information on them. Gang members came to the library to vandalize the building or tag the books with their graffiti, recruit other kids or shake them down for money, sell drugs, or steal purses, phones, and tablets. Teenagers have sex in the secluded areas. Neglectful parents drop off too-young kids for twelve hours. Alleged caregivers roll their wheelchair-bound or elderly patients to a table, give them a book, and then leave for ten hours. The homeless eat, sleep, and panhandle in the library and take sink showers in the restrooms. People bring into the branches "comfort animals," not trained dogs for the blind or disabled, but snakes, ferrets, parrots, turtles, and rats. In the San Francisco Civic Center branch and the main downtown City of Los Angeles libraries, the uniformed security staff members post pictures in their guard offices of the worst offenders, thieves, and sexual predators.

I have heard your stories. The common thread is that these patrons and the situations they create make your working lives miserable, bother other library customers, and raise liability concerns.

Nevertheless, challenging people need your best efforts to serve their needs. This book will help you feel more comfortable around uncomfortable people. It discusses creative patron communication methods and what I define as "high-risk customer service tools" for behaviors that raise the stakes. In law enforcement, we used the Rule of Three to get compliance from uncooperative people: Ask. Tell. Make. You have the ability to use the first two. A challenging patron's interaction with you, another staff member, or another patron may become so problematic that you need to call the cops for the third. This book will help you decide if you've reached that point.

I wrote this book with every library worker in mind as a potential reader. If you're a frontline library employee, then you can use this book to make suggestions to your coworkers and bosses in staff meetings, training discussions, and other formal or informal conversations about how to keep things safe.

Courage is a learned skill, and one I admire. I like library directors with the courage to do the right thing, and I have seen many examples of this. They take ownership and defend their right to create a safe, functioning, peaceful place to work and visit. If you're in charge of people or facilities, use this book as a road map to make the changes your experience, intuition, contextual circumstances, and interactions between patrons and employees at your branch have been telling you to initiate. This book will help you create and maintain the kind of security-driven environment that will improve employee morale, enhance employee retention, and polish employee interactions with all patrons.

Admittedly, I still think like a cop. I tend to view things in the library as either safe or not safe, secure or not secure. I realize there are gray areas when it comes to human behavior, but I'm perhaps less forgiving of the rude, angry, eccentric, entitled, or threatening patron than you might be. What you are willing to tolerate, because of librarianship's principles of access or simply because you see these same people day after day, may be different. Differing perspectives aside, my goal for this book is to encourage you in all situations to enforce your codes of conduct, policies, and standards for all people using the library in a way that is firm, fair, consistent, and assertive.

I've included some additional material in appendixes at the end of the book, including a checklist for conducting a security assessment of your facility, several staff training exercises you can do as part of ongoing staff development or just as a way to spice up a staff meeting, and a helpful primer on employee stress management.

Most libraries call me to set up a training workshop or to consult on a dangerous or threatening patron issue only when the situation has become unbearable. My knowledge of the context and history of a patron's past behaviors is limited. My objective is to guide you in getting the patron to cooperate, to leave quietly or noisily, but without hurting anybody. I may suggest some tools, approaches, or solutions that seem unusual, outside the box, and even manipulative. I ask that you keep an open mind and try every conversational or positional tool (e.g., space, distance, barriers). Apply the best ideas to the patrons and situations that you face, evaluate your successes, and keep on keeping on.

I often ask workshop participants if our goal when dealing with problematic patrons should be Peace or Justice. I usually get the right answer: Peace. Justice is rare, hard to define, and not always possible. Peace is possible. Use your best customer service skills, treat the person with respect even when it's difficult, consider your best actions for the safety and security of everyone in the room, and help the person leave feeling relatively satisfied that you did the best you could for him or her. Go for Peace.

ACKNOWLEDGMENTS

My work in libraries is greatly enhanced by the support of professional librarians around the country who have shared their security concerns, educated me on the daily operations at their facilities, and allowed me to talk to their staffs in ways that helped us all.

My particular thanks go to the City of Carlsbad (CA) Library, Library Director Heather Pizzuto, and her senior staff members for their longtime faith and support.

Cheryl Gould, now a library training consultant at www.fullyengaged libraries.com, brought me into the library world through her work in California as the Director of Training for Infopeople.org.

Catherine Hakala-Ausperk, at www.librariesthrive.com, is a great resource and ALA presenting partner.

I have benefited from my relationships with these library directors and their staffs:

City of San Diego (CA) Public Library and now-retired Library Director Deborah Barrow

County of San Diego (CA) Library

San Francisco (CA) Public Library and former Volunteer Services Director Paul Signorelli, who also introduced me to Dan Freeman and the good folks at the American Library Association

City of Los Angeles (CA) Library

County of Los Angeles (CA) Library

County of Los Angeles (CA) Law Library

City of Oakland (CA) Library

City of San José (CA) Library

City of Baltimore (MD) Library

County of Baltimore (MD) Library

County of San Luis Obispo (CA) Library and John Schwind, County Safety Officer

Solano County (CA) Library and Bonnie Kolesar, Risk Manager

Mendocino County (CA) Library and General Services Agency Director Kristin McMenomey

City of South Pasadena (CA) Library and Library Director Steve Fjelsted

City of Oxnard (CA) Library and Library Director Barbara Murray

City of Sacramento (CA) Library

City of Riverside (CA) Law Library

City of Palm Springs (CA) Library

City of Fresno (CA) Library

City of Escondido (CA) Library

City of Chula Vista (CA) Library

City of Vista (CA) Library

City of El Cajon (CA) Library

City of Watsonville (CA) Library

City of Carmel (CA) Library

City of Palo Alto (CA) Library

City of Berkeley (CA) Library

City of Mountain View (CA) Library

City of Covina (CA) Library

City of Ventura (CA) Library

City of Vallejo (CA) Library

County of Tehama (CA) Library

City of Cerritos (CA) Library

City of San Bernardino (CA) Library

City of Santa Cruz (CA) Library

City of Poway (CA) Library

City of Woodland (CA) Library

City of Buena Park (CA) Library

CHAPTER 1

The New Library Workplace

Not So Quiet

A patron has been occupying an Internet computer for several hours and is pulling up one adult site after another; patrons with nearby children are starting to complain. An angry woman comes in with her fourteen-year-old son to ask you why he was kicked out of the library yesterday (which was your day off). An elderly man has a lot of fines and missing materials; he wants to check out too many items and he gets upset when he is told he cannot. Two teenagers are making out in the library; other patrons are uncomfortable. A seven-year-old seems lost in the library; it looks like one of his erstwhile parents may have dropped him off for the whole day. A homeless man, one of your regulars, is asking highly personal questions of the female staff and female patrons, including young girls. A man is talking loudly on his cell phone, while eating a greasy sandwich at the periodicals table; when you come over, he starts with, "Don't you dare bother me! My taxes pay your salary!"

And so begins another working day at your library. Large or small facility, rural or urban location, law or university or city or county library, lots of branches or one, many employees on-site or only a few—these situations are common, distracting, and potentially troubling.

You thought this job was about the great books, history on the page, and having the time to review the periodicals and publications that interest you. In reality, it's really about people, and sometimes those people are odd, demanding, entitled, angry, or even threatening. The nature of the beast in many libraries is having to deal with, on an occasional or a regular basis, eccentric people.

Patron behavior problems are not new to libraries, but there are certainly new solutions, ranging from bringing in liaison partners like homeless advocates, police task forces, or adult or child protective services officials, to the use of temporary restraining orders (TROs), regular staff meetings about security issues, better door locks, and restroom redesigns. You can have the library you want to work in and patrons want to visit. However, what you want and what you might get can be quite different.

The December 13, 2010, edition of *USA Today* ran a front-page headline story (by staff writer Judy Keen), below the fold, that either struck fear in the hearts of library people or, more likely, caused them to shake their heads at another sign of the times: "Libraries welcome the homeless. Some start book clubs or show movies for patrons." This short article verified what most library supervisors and their employees already knew (and what some taxpayers and library patrons know too): While some libraries continue to fight the good daily fight by trying to minimize the negative impact of disruptive homeless people, others have thrown in the towel.

Some facilities have adopted the coping philosophy espoused by San Francisco City Librarian Luis Herrera: "Libraries are becoming our community living rooms." His facility employs a psychiatric social worker, who helps the homeless who enter the San Francisco Civic Center branch with referrals to city resources. (As a side note, that branch has a beautiful rotunda near the entrance. Staffers who see the mentally ill homeless congregate underneath this dome day after day, week after week, and year after year have dubbed it "Area 51.")

When library employees get frustrated with their patrons and vice versa, two common themes emerge, one from the patrons and one from the staffers. From the patrons: "I miss the 'old' library. Where's the card catalog?" "How come people can eat and talk on their phones here? I miss the quiet." "It wasn't like this in the good old days." When I teach my library safety and security workshops around the country, these are the three most common complaints from library staffers: "This would be a great place to work if it weren't for all these entitled patrons." "This would be a great place to work if we didn't have patrons misusing or fighting over the Internet here." "This would be a great place to work if people respected library staff like they did when I was a kid." Sound familiar? Even the most positive library people— and I've met many in my travels—have to admit that it ain't your mom and dad's library anymore.

Have libraries had to reposition themselves to stay relevant? Of course. Will libraries have to continue to offer new approaches, to attract newer patrons, beyond just students, the elderly—who see the library as a community necessity—and those adults who have always used and liked libraries, and their children? Yes again.

And in terms of patron behavior problems, has the library gotten worse, has it always been bad, or is it mostly tolerable, with a few challenging people on an irregular basis? Of course, this depends on who you ask. Some staffers work in libraries located in tough, gritty, high-crime neighborhoods, where the facility draws some scary or dangerous people on a daily basis. Others work in similar cities where the library is seen as a neutral zone, so the bad guys tend to stay out. Other library people work in more remote or rural libraries and are fearful of certain patrons because they may be the only person on duty in a tiny branch. These patrons are scary, intimidating, and frequently have no place else to go in that small town, so they hold court at the library and act out regularly. Police response to these locations is spotty or from a distance, or both. At least those staff members who work in big cities with lots of crime have the advantage of having lots of cops nearby (even if they don't ever come by unless they're called for a real emergency).

Regardless of where you work, you will have to deal with the changing nature of patrons today, which means more mental illness with some of them, more substance abuse, more kids with behavior problems—left alone in the library by parents who leave them for hours—and plenty of boundary-pushing behaviors by the entitled, who don't believe your rules or codes of conduct ever apply to them.

This book exists to make you feel confident about going to work each day, more empowered to make good decisions on behalf of your facility, your boss, and your colleagues, and to help you help those patrons who have a sense of respect for you and the function of a library. Throughout this book, you're encouraged to use your intuition in those situations where you need to make immediate decisions as to what to say or do and, just as important, what not to say or do. By saying, "Listen, pal, if I have to tell you one more time to stop doing that, there's going to be trouble" and then not enforcing any consequences, you've just made the situation worse.

You have the right to question my methods or suggestions in this book. Some of them will work for you, in your facility, and for the situations you're facing. You may have to try some of them more than once because the people you're encountering just don't listen or hear you or care to comply. You have the right to try, try, try, and then disengage and get help. You have the right to work in the safest environment you and your colleagues can create.

Comments from Library Staffers around the Nation

Here's what your Brothers and Sisters of the Book are saying about the difficulty of their work environments and problematic patrons.

From a staffer at the US Library of Congress regarding the Internet: "This kind of behavior happens even in our national library. The computer center is a magnet for the homeless, the mentally unstable, and porn addicts, among others. Your tax dollars at work. I've seen homeless men having nearly naked sink baths in the restrooms. There are a great many of these regulars who arrive when the doors open at 8:30 a.m. and don't leave until they're asked to leave at closing time. There have been near fistfights among several competing mentally unstable people and people taken out in handcuffs. Librarians have access to panic buttons that summon squads of police when needed."

According to a library branch manager in San Diego County, "Most people are nice and courteous; however, there is a bit of desperation in patrons trying to get résumés and applications out in a timely manner. Some patrons get upset a little faster than they used to. We have a lot of issues with unsupervised teens pushing the limits."

When asked if the struggling economy in her City of Oakland (CA) library has had an impact on worsening patron behaviors, a longtime staffer said, "I don't think that it has made it any worse. Those who are rude and/or hostile continue to be that way. We do have an increased volume of business, especially those seeking work and applying for unemployment. Many of these people have no computer skills and need more help than we can provide, leading to frustration for them."

From a Baltimore County (MD) library staffer: "The most common security issues we see at our facility are patrons stealing materials, especially CDs and DVDs; fighting over computer access; and inappropriate behavior due to their intoxication. We have had to get temporary restraining orders against patrons who continually harassed staff or other patrons, stared at people, or threatened staff. We try to get support from our law enforcement agencies, but their responses are not always timely."

Do any of these concerns sound familiar to you?

Our Motto

Perhaps it helps to start with a theme that bypasses the *why* of patron behavior problems and focuses more on the *how*.

> We can accept the person without having to accept his or her inappropriate behavior.

In my work, I'm often asked if a person who commits an act of violence somehow fits a "profile" of a violent perpetrator. (This is a popular question from those in the media, who keep grasping for the perfect characteristics of active shooters in schools and workplaces, which just don't exist.) The truth is that many angry people, when confronted with a problem they don't know how to solve, can resort to violence—young or old, male or female, any race, any religion, with or without a criminal history. Assuming this is true, and significant and voluminous research from the US Marshals, Federal Bureau of Investigation (FBI), and Secret Service suggests that it is, then we can skip the search for a collection of demographic characteristics and focus our energy and prevention attentions on patron *behaviors*.

Related to the never-ending search for profiles that don't exist is the futility of looking for a motive as to why people act up or act out using violence. There are many reasons why people, even mostly peaceable types, act out with violence, including mental illness, irrational religious beliefs, a broken heart, the chemical imbalances brought on by substance abuse, uncontrollable rage that comes from a frontal lobe brain injury, or a perceived and skewed sense of personal injustice. The bad news in all of this is that we can't always understand these motives or prevent them. Some horribly violent perpetrators took their reasons with them to the grave; others described them in great detail through their notes, blogs, or other social media postings.

The better news is that while we can't control people's behaviors, we can control our perception of them, our responses to them, and, ultimately, our treatment of them. So the rest of this book focuses on behaviors, not profiles, and our responses to those patron behaviors which hurt the library experience for other people and the staff.

The New Library Environment?

It's possible that some patrons feel a bit overwhelmed and even a little power-less in the so-called "new library." To wit: "I miss the 'old library.' Where is the card catalog?" they ask themselves or you. "People can buy coffee and scones here and eat them in the stacks?" they say, looking around as an espresso machine whirs in the background. "How do I look up a book using the computer system? Do they still use the Dewey Decimal System here?" "The library website sure has a lot of stuff on it, but it's a little hard to navigate." "They have this self-service checkout machine that I can't figure out and don't want to. I like talking to the people who work here, but they always seem to want to direct me over to all these new technologies. I miss the human touch." Before you chalk up these complaints to some senior citizens who are deathly fearful of computers, recognize that these comments have come from patrons of all ages, even those who consider themselves tech savvy.

And how about library staffers who miss the "old library"? Here's what they have to say:

> "Back in the day, people were quiet. You could hear yourself think. Now we have to listen to people playing videos on their cell phones at full volume without using headphones."

> "We are expected to be able to answer a lot of tech questions about how to connect our patrons and their tablets to our Wi-Fi system. Everyone has a different system and it's just as confusing to us as it is to them. They think we should know everything about their devices."

> "The homeless population seems more aggressive, more mentally ill, and more entitled than ever before. They quote our policies to us, the Penal Code, and they seem to know a lot better than we do as to when we can or cannot ask them to leave."

> "A lot of patrons don't know our rules, don't plan to learn them, or ignore our rules, because we seem to have the same conversations about what they can and can't do, every time they come here."

> "We seem to get a lot of grief from our elected officials. We ask a patron to comply with a policy or kick them out for bothering

people and they go straight to our library director or to a city council member to complain. We end up getting called on the carpet for trying to do our jobs. I wish our library director would take our side more often. Once an elected official gets involved, you can guarantee the problem patron is coming back here and will feel pretty self-satisfied about it."

"There is a general lack of respect between people. Patrons are rude to each other and to staff. Staff feel disrespected so they give it right back sometimes. Patrons come in angry and leave that way, especially when we can't solve their problems the way they think we should."

"We feel like we have to do more, with less help, and faster than ever before. Budget money is tight. We're not hiring extra people and we're not even replacing the employees who retire or leave. Employees are under stress here."

This is not to suggest that we should post a sign over the staff entrance of every library in the country that reads, "Abandon hope all ye who enter here." But even the most cheerful library director or the most optimistic and humanistic library employee will have to admit that the library world is becoming a tougher environment.

"When Do I Do What I Know I Should Do?"

At some early point in my library workshops, a participant will approach me in a hesitant and almost sheepish manner. It usually happens on the first break (and when I'm desperately seeking the men's room). This person will say, "Can I tell you about a situation that happened here? I want to know if I did the right thing."

He or she will tell me a story about an angry, difficult, entitled, or threatening patron and what he or she did to handle the person. This may involve using what I define as high-risk communication skills, calling over another colleague for help, bringing in a supervisor to take over as a near last resort, completely disengaging from the patron because of a threat, or even calling the police to have the patron escorted out or arrested. (A variation of this question is, "Are you going to talk about when it's the right time to get help or get out of there or call the police because of a scary patron?")

Of course, these employees are looking for validation, support, and even praise from me, all of which I give by the handful because, in the majority of examples they tell me, they did exactly the right thing. I rarely have any argument with how they handled their situations. I offer words of encouragement, suggest some fine-tuning for a similar situation next time, and try to send them back to their chairs feeling empowered.

This leads me to think about the answer to their ultimate question: "When do I do what I know I should do?" (Say that three times fast after you've had a few adult beverages.) I think the answer to this question is that there are multiple answers, based on both the content and the context of the situation. Following are some examples of when you need to step in and enforce your code of conduct and behavioral policies, either alone, with one or more colleagues to support you, using help from your boss, or requesting a police response.

When It Hurts Your Business

There are lots of examples of situations in which a patron's behavior is irritating (like a patron cutting fingernails at a table and sweeping the clippings onto the floor while packing up to leave) but does not necessarily impact the business of being a library in a negative way. A parent changing an infant's dirty diaper on the tray table on the airplane may be gross, but it doesn't affect the way the pilot operates the controls. However, when the behavior or antics of a patron disrupt the business of the library, that is your signal to address the problem.

This is a contextual issue, one that has to do with your level of patience for something that a coworker might think is a huge deal while you don't, or vice versa. There is no perfect answer for whether you should or should not talk to a patron. Some library employees let homeless people sleep in the library as long as they are not blocking the way of wide-awake patrons or snoring loudly enough to be heard outside. For others, this is a major pet peeve, and they spend their days rousing the snoozers. Some library staff members put kids and teens on a very short leash when it comes to disruptive behaviors while others say, "Let kids be kids."

Other factors will play into your decision, including the current culture at your library; the level of tolerance, as displayed by the director and senior staff; previous incidents or accidents, especially those which resulted in dollar losses, payouts, or pending litigation; the neighborhood; the level of patience, concern, or apathy exhibited by other patrons; and the influence of a library board, Friends of the Library group, city or county officials, your municipal attorneys, and/or elected officials.

When Your Intuition Kicks In

In his best-selling book *The Gift of Fear: Survival Signals That Protect Us from Violence* (Little, Brown, 1997), Hollywood celebrity security expert Gavin de Becker calls intuition both a powerful force and "a unique form of knowing." He reminds us that it's *always* in response to something you see, hear, or, more likely, feel. It *always* acts in your best interests (and we all have examples of when this was true). We all have examples of when following our intuitive feelings worked and of how it hurt when we didn't follow them. And, as de Becker cautions, human beings are the *only* creatures on the planet who override their intuitive feelings. Animals don't do this in nature because they know it might lead to their deaths. No smart gazelle continues drinking at the water hole after hearing the crunch of paw steps over his shoulder. If the little voice in your head says, "I wonder if I should walk over there and mention something to that patron?," then do so. If the little voice says, "Should I go and get my boss for help?," then do that. If the little voice says, "I think I had better go call the cops," then don't ignore your concern; it's trying to keep you and others safe. (If you hear more than one little voice, seek psychiatric help.)

When Other Patrons Complain or Are Afraid

Some patrons are vocal about what they see as bad things going on in *their* library. They may ask you to address a patron's behavior problem while standing five feet from that person, almost as if they are challenging you to "do your job" in front of them. This can put added stress on you and create a new, additional conflict between those two patrons. Other patrons may approach you more quietly to point out a situation that is occurring with which they need your help.

When Other Coworkers Complain or Are Afraid

An example of this happens at staff meetings when the behavior of one of your "frequent fliers" comes up yet again. Instead of shrugging your collective shoulders and saying, "Well, what can we do?" about someone who repeatedly does the same things to disrupt the business, come up with a plan and put it into action the next time he or she does it again. If a patron scares you and/or other coworkers, it's important to talk about the solution and activate it.

When You Know You Need to Set Limits and Boundaries, Now and for the Future

Problem patrons will try only what they think they can get away with. I preach the need to be consistent throughout this book. If people think they can eat or sleep or pester other people for money and you will not address their actions, then they will continue to behave in these ways. And not only do you need to address this situation; your colleagues need to back your play, when they are on the floor with you and, especially, when you aren't there. Problem patrons learn quickly which staffers will make them follow the rules and which won't, and they adjust their library visits accordingly.

When the Situation Fails the "Reasonable Employee" Test

You will see the term *reasonable* pop up in any number of civil court cases or in the descriptions of laws, especially those related to employment or any event involving a strong difference of opinion between two parties: Was the employer reasonable in its response to the issue when it surfaced? Did the employee take reasonable steps to address the situation when he or she encountered it? Did the supervisor respond reasonably? Was the police response necessary and reasonable? You should always ask yourself, "Am I being reasonable in my response to this patron's behavior? Am I overreacting or underreacting? What would another library professional like me do in a similar situation?"

Are Your Problem Patrons Yes, Maybe, or No People?

In many situations involving patrons, it helps to first assess their perceived levels of cooperation. Are they *yes* people, meaning you always get a good, cooperative response from them when they are asked to comply? Are they *maybe* people who maybe will cooperate and maybe won't, depending on their mood or, more likely, how you treat them when you ask? Or are they *no* people who won't cooperate, no matter how nicely you ask?

I used this approach plenty in my policing career, usually making the decision in the first few moments after my arrival. *Yes* people left when I asked and did not scream or yell or argue that they were right and I was dead wrong. *Maybe* people usually cooperated once they realized they were on thin ice in terms of choices. *No* people usually required me to call for backup and would help me get a torn uniform before they finally gave up.

The key to this model is knowing that sometimes, either accidentally or intentionally, you can turn *yes* people into *no* people based on how you treat or mistreat them (at least in their eyes). You can turn a cooperative person into a screaming maniac by being condescending, rude, or officious with him or her.

Don't Rationalize Irrational Behavior

Think of the number of times you have said the following when faced with a difficult, rude, challenging, obnoxious, or even threatening patron who does something on a one-time or continuing basis that puts you and other patrons at risk:

"I'm probably overreacting..."

"I'll stop it if he or she does *x*, *y*, or *z*..."

"They'll go away soon, I hope..."

"Maybe if I just wait her out..."

"It's not really that bad..."

"It's not my job to handle that..."

"My supervisor is on a break..."

"I'm not a cop, psychologist, or social worker..."

"Asking for help means I can't do my job..."

"This is not bad enough for me to call the police yet..."

There is no value to rationalizing what you know is the right thing to do. You already know that this conversation in your head goes against your intuitive feelings, and it only delays you from doing what you know you should do.

Nothing that follows in this book about dealing with difficult, challenging, confrontational, or high-risk patrons says you have to deal with them alone. We will talk about maximizing your resources and making it easy for you to have hard conversations as we go forward.

CHAPTER 2

Three Keys to a Safer Library

Security-Aware Staff, Creative Customer Service Skills, and Enforced Codes of Conduct

The following theme appears throughout the book (you should be able to recite it from memory by the end):

> Every library employee will pay attention to his or her own safety and the safety of his or her colleagues. Every employee will strive to provide great customer service to all patrons, even when those patrons are challenging or difficult. And every employee will work together to make certain the code of conduct is enforced in ways that are firm, fair, consistent, and assertive.

This is an empathetic model for service excellence and one in which the consistent application of library policies and codes of conduct can go a long way toward creating more uniform responses to and for patrons and toward having the library be a safe place to visit and an enjoyable place to work.

Safety and Security Themes

When I ask library people, "Who is in charge of safety and security for your library?," the most common answer is, "The police department or sheriff's department." Some people will say, "The library director," and a few brave souls will give me the correct answer: "Everyone who works here and even the patrons. We're all in charge of safety and security, just like in this nation and in our communities."

Safety and security at work is everyone's job. This includes the library director, every department head, every supervisor, all full-time and part-time employees, library board members, Friends of the Library group members, elected officials, and even patrons, who can and should tell us about safety or security situations we need to address when they are using our branches. There are not enough police or sheriff's deputies to take care of every single situation. We must use them wisely and for those incidents for which their specific type of expertise is required. The rest is on our shoulders.

Since it's a part of all of our job duties, we must agree to take care of one another here by being *proactive*. That doesn't mean we go around looking for problems that aren't there or creating confrontations with patrons in an attempt to turn the library into a place that's too strict about the rules and no fun to visit.

Facility safety and security is a big responsibility and an important one; we're talking about people's lives here. And since we know we already live in a world where crime and conflict and violence are real possibilities, it helps to have some absolutes when it comes to our methods and approaches to keeping staff and patrons safe. I suggest these five:

- We will treat all patrons with respect, even and especially when we disagree with their behavior. We won't use "profiles" about threatening, dangerous, or violent people because they don't exist. We will accept all patrons, without having to accept their inappropriate behaviors.
- Our library organization won't tolerate crimes, threats, or acts of workplace violence. We won't wait for events to make smart security improvements. Security and safety at our facilities is a work in progress.
- There should be consequences for patrons, outsiders, or criminals who violate the law, our codes of conduct, and our safety and security policies.
- We will offer support and assistance for every employee and every patron who asks for or needs help with safety or security concerns, including bringing in law enforcement.
- As to our work culture, we will agree that employees' asking for help does not mean they don't know how to do their jobs with

patrons; it just means they need help at that moment. And we will ask all staff to do their jobs safely, not just do their jobs. There's a critical difference between the two.

Degrees of Alertness

When you're watching out for one another and keeping safety in mind, you are in what I call Condition Yellow. This does not refer to some kind of rare tropical fever but simply to your ability to pay attention to your safety and security anytime you're on the library floor, in the stacks, at the service desk, in transit between the floors of your facility, entering or leaving your facility, or in view of or in contact with the public. Condition Yellow represents the everyday level of alertness that you use in your job, but you should keep in mind the other two security levels: Condition White and Condition Red.

Perhaps it's best to view Condition White along a spectrum. It serves its purpose when you are on a break, in the back office where it is safe, eating your lunch, chatting with colleagues, or safely behind the scenes and otherwise not actively engaged with patrons or other strangers. In those instances, Condition White means relax, catch your breath, and regenerate your energy to finish the day with as much of the same useful stamina as when you arrived. The other end of the Condition White spectrum is when you are caught unaware by a situation or a patron's behavior because you weren't paying attention and didn't consider the possibility that he or she would erupt. The operant phrases for the not-good Condition White are these: "What just happened?" "I didn't see that coming." "I was caught off guard."

Here's an example of Condition White in action: I live in a small mountain town east of San Diego, California. We're big enough to have a Starbucks, but not big enough to have two. On a regular basis, I will watch men and women drive into the Starbucks parking lot, park their expensive SUV or fancy truck, leave the engine running, and dash into the coffee shop to get their favorite iced or steaming beverage. When they return to their (quite expensive) vehicle with the keys still in the ignition, everything is fine, they hop in, and drive off. However, I can't help thinking that sometime an enterprising young car thief will jump into their $45,000 automobile and drive away with it, thanking them silently for making it so easy.

Condition White is when you make mistakes about interpreting people, safety, or security based on what Hollywood security expert Gavin de

Becker calls "The Myth of No Past Problems." This myth gets its label from the fallacy that because yesterday was boring at work, today will be boring at work; because the last time I dealt with this patron he or she was cooperative, he or she will be just as cooperative again today.

Condition Red gives you two choices: Get out of the dangerous situation immediately or, if necessary, protect yourself by fighting back. I prefer the first to the second, as I'm sure your supervisor, library director, HR representative, municipal attorneys, or joint powers insurance carrier does as well, but I'm not discounting the need to protect yourself physically. The majority of the discussions in this book are for what I call "psychological self-defense"—how to outwit, outthink, outmaneuver, or outtalk difficult people. But the book also covers (briefly) how to protect yourself physically since there is a time to talk and a time to move away smartly or protect yourself, as any reasonable person should do. Many people have done brave and heroic things to protect themselves when faced with violence and lived to tell about it, even if they originally had thought they never could.

Three Core Values for a Safer Workplace

These three elements—self-protection, anger and stress management, and working smart—are certainly important when viewed alone, but in combination, they can work to keep you safer (and saner) while you interact with patrons.

Self-Protection

You can't take care of others if you're not safe from harm. When you are working around people you don't know, it always makes good security sense to stay at least arm's length away from them until you feel more comfortable coming a bit closer. When people feel crowded, they often react with anger, so give people their space, especially if you see that they are starting to get upset.

It's also important to stay out of the face-to-face zone with angry people. Phrases like "He got in my face" and "She got in my space" exist for a reason. Try to approach angry people at a slight angle, just to the side of either of their shoulders.

You can use proxemic barriers when dealing with hostile people. Proxemics has to do with that bubble of space we all carry around ourselves.

We engage with most people using "social space." We use "personal space" around our friends and people we know, like, and trust. We let people we love into our "intimate space." To limit angry people from accessing our physical space, we can use available proxemic barriers, like tables, counters, chairs, windows, and even the telephone ("No need to come down here, sir. We'll e-mail you what you need").

Read situations with angry or entitled patrons by examining their tone, facial expressions, and body language for signs that they feel deeply embarrassed, humiliated, and/or disrespected; maybe there are no good solutions or you see escalating anger or sudden rage. In these events, their next response is often to use violence, and when that happens, you have every right to disengage, physically leave the situation, and go get help, including calling the police. You can't just walk away if a patron raises his or her left eyebrow at you, but you are under no obligation to stand at your desk or on the library floor and wait to be assaulted either. Justify why you left and got help after the situation has stabilized.

Anger Management and Stress Management

You can't take care of others or yourself if you're losing it. As my customer service training colleagues like to remind me, when it comes to dealing with difficult or challenging patrons, who may use mean words to try to degrade you, your job, or your efforts, always remember QTIP: Quit Taking It Personally. The majority of the time, angry or entitled patrons aren't mad at you personally; they're mad at who or what you represent—an employee of a public space entity that has rules, a code of conduct, and policies they find irritating, chafing, or not meant for them.

It's just business; don't take bad encounters with equally bad patrons home with you inside your head. If they ruin a night of sleep for you, then they win, which is not what you need or want. They don't have the right to abuse, threaten, or harm you, but you will have to use your patience, perspective, and customer service skills at all times when dealing with every patron in general and for those problematic patrons in particular.

The best way to manage your personal stress, either throughout your day or especially when dealing with demanding, entitled, angry, or threatening people, is to control your breathing. ("You aren't going to give us a lesson on how to breathe, are you, Steve? We've all been breathing for many years." Yes, I am.) Stressful breathing is short, shallow, and anxious. It raises your pulse rate and blood pressure to uncomfortable levels. When you're in the fight-or-flight mode that comes during stressful breathing, you can create a vicious cycle: The shorter your breaths, the more of them you need to take. Without good oxygen control, your body shifts into fight-or-flight mode faster than you want. You get tunnel vision and tunnel hearing, as the blood leaves your brain and moves to your extremities. All of this makes it harder for you to think, speak, and act effectively.

In contrast, stress management breathing is slow, deep, and calming. Practice this when things are calm around you and you have a moment of transition: Inhale deeply, hold it for a second or two, and then exhale deeply, hold it for second or two, and start the next inhalation. Repeat for about twenty breaths and you will see instant results as your pace slows and the environment around you clarifies. Make this your mantra: "The more out of control the situation is, the more I need to control my breathing." (Appendix D offers some additional material for you on stress management.)

Working Smart

This last concept asks you to know what to say, what to do, when to stay or go, who to call, and how to get help when dealing with challenging patrons. Getting help is no sin and is not a reflection of your customer service skills as an employee or a library professional. Most times you can use good communication skills to solve a patron's problem; sometimes you just need to get another employee or supervisor with a different approach.

Think about this concept of "the right person for the right patron in the right situation at the right time" as an *alignment* of sorts. Human beings align and connect with one another for a variety of reasons, including race, age, gender, religion, country of origin, neighborhoods, hobbies, and lifestyles. You can use this concept to your advantage in service situations by trading off with one another based on who gets along with the approaching patron the best. You've certainly seen this many times in your career. A patron comes in who seems to like you but hates your coworker's purple guts, or here comes the patron who can't stand you, and tells you so, but seems to connect with your colleague in a way that's both obvious and a clear signal for you step away and let them interact. Once you figure this out with your colleagues, you can start "trading off" with them for those patrons who seem to align best with each of you. It's not always possible to do this, but when it is, you can choose to go with the patron's flow instead of trying to swim upstream.

My first understanding of the critical importance of alignment came when I interviewed double workplace violence murderer Robert Mack in a California prison in 1993 for my *Ticking Bombs* book. Mack told me he was a twenty-five-year employee of his company, General Dynamics, when he was fired by a labor relations manager who was twenty-five years old. In his depressed and angry mental state at the time of his termination, he took this to be a great insult. How dare the company send a guy who was in diapers when Mack started working there to fire him? Who knows whether bringing in a longtime HR executive to handle his termination hearing would have made any difference in "aligning" his emotional state and thereby prevented him from shooting two people, but the possibility is certainly worth considering.

A key component of working smart is your ability to document bad behavior, using an informal memo or e-mail to your boss or a more formal approach, like filling out a Security Incident Report. Here's one example where after-the-fact documentation can help protect your professional reputation: You are speaking on the phone to an increasingly angry patron who starts cursing at you. You warn him once that he can't speak to you this way if he expects you to help him and tell him that if he continues, you'll hang up. If he keeps cursing, keep your promise (firm, fair, consistent, assertive) and hang up. Take a few stress management breaths and then document the conversation, including the actual curse words, verbatim.

Here's why: When this type of patron calls back to complain to your supervisor or, better yet, shows up in person to meet with your library director, he or she is often wearing a shiny halo and a set of tiny angel wings. This is what the director will hear: "I've never been treated like that in all my years!" or "I was shocked, insulted, embarrassed, and now I'm thinking of speaking to my lawyer." It's important to depict accurately exactly what the person said—not just "He cursed at me" but what specifically was said—to help your boss justify why you did what you did in light of what the patron said. Your boss should say, "My report indicates you called our employee a 'stupid mother@!#$&%' at least twice. We don't allow our employees to continue with the call at that point."

Making Safety, Security, and Service Rules Work

- Know that a good predictor of future bad patron behavior is past bad patron behavior.
- If you impose no consequences for a problem behavior, expect it to stay the same or escalate.
- Don't trade security for convenience. Lock employees-only doors, protect yourself and your colleagues, and use your security devices, policies, and procedures.
- Don't rationalize irrational patron behaviors.
- Don't ignore safety or security problems; they rarely go away.
- Listen carefully to your colleagues and the patrons as they explain their view of a situation.
- Avoid snap decisions unless it's an emergency situation. Assess several possible responses before you make a decision.
- As best as you can, stay focused and nonjudgmental; don't lose your patience or your temper or become fearful, as these hurt your decision-making process.
- Paraphrase what you hear back to the patron until you both agree on what the problem is.
- When you understand what the problem is, take action, if you can, to resolve it quickly by valuing the patron's time.
- Explain your position using firm, fair, consistent, and assertive language.
- Keep your tone neutral and polite. Take special care not to use a condescending tone, especially when you're tired or frustrated or at the end of your day.
- Use the power of your colleagues to work as a team on particularly difficult patron situations.
- Get outside help, support, and advice if necessary, especially from your stakeholders in safety and security (police or sheriff's department, HR, city attorney, county counsel, risk management personnel, facilities staff).
- After a particularly difficult patron situation, debrief, support, and praise one other when it's safe to do so.

Customer Service Realities: Starting with You

It's no secret that library work draws introverted employees. You may define yourself as being an introvert trapped in an extrovert's profession, as do I. Each week, somewhere in the United States, I stand in front of total strangers and talk, often for many hours, all day. Since I routinely engage in a behavior that causes fear in even the bravest souls—public speaking—I must gear up for my work as if for an onstage performance because it feels like I'm acting in a play. Fortunately, since I wrote the play and I know when and how to say all the lines, I'm comfortable doing this.

You may feel like you're onstage every time you leave the relative comfort and safety of the back office and start interacting with patrons. It can help to see your work in a public contact job as a bit of a performance for several reasons: You can step a bit outside yourself and focus on your role as a professional information-providing specialist; you can shift on the fly and adjust both your responses and your reactions to the different patrons who make demands on you when they are rude, abrupt, demanding, eccentric, officious, obnoxious, stressed out by life, or just in a huge hurry; and you can learn to QTIP.

To quote my dad, Karl Albrecht, an author of several best-selling books on customer service: "Good service is about good feelings. It's more than just smiling or being friendly; it's an attitude that comes from wanting to help people from the moment they arrive." Some people wrongly interpret this idea as having to be subservient to others or somehow sacrifice your personality by bowing down or kissing up to people, especially when it's not what you feel like doing. This is an incorrect perspective. Professional service providers take pride in what they do; they enjoy a lot of their work, even if they are introverts by nature.

Customer contact, taxpayer contact, or patron contact jobs demand that you make yourself available to people and not bend to their will, allow them to ride roughshod over you, or be mistreated. Consider the best service people you've ever encountered. Maybe it was at a hotel, a restaurant, or over the phone with your bank or an airline. The encounters had common characteristics: The service people made you feel important; they were real and spoke to you like another human being, not like a robot; they didn't use canned speeches or countless apologies when things went wrong; they took ownership and solved your problem; they valued your time; and they probably added some small bonus at the end that made it all come together correctly.

Do you want to know how they were able to provide you with excellent service, even giving you something unexpected, beyond just the basic human pleasantries? They faked it. Yes, you read that correctly. Skilled service people know that they don't always come to work at peak energy. They know that they have some days when they wake up feeling like the wrong end of the dog. They get just as frustrated with customers and tired of working in their respective bureaucracies as you do. Their secret is not letting it show.

Sometimes when it comes to dealing with angry, entitled, eccentric, impatient, rude, or demanding patrons, you have to fake it. I don't mean being insincere; I mean gearing up for your daily performance like you were an actor or an actress in a play. When you see a play or a musical or an opera or any live performance, including standup comedy, you know those performers have said those same lines hundreds of times. It may be the 353rd time for them, but they know it's probably the first time for you. You should approach your patrons in the same way. The library branch is your world, not theirs. You know every inch and you know how to do your job because you've already done it for months, years, or decades.

Service jobs can be challenging. If you have a high human contact job and low control over the work you do, it's easy to get bored, look bored, sound bored, go home tired, or even want to quit. The more transactional— as in repetitive—your job is, the more you have to find ways to do it that make it interesting for you. Even if you do the same tasks over and over (and over), it's new to your patrons. First time for them but not the first time for you—act just like you were being paid to perform, because you are.

Great Customer Service over the Phone

Over the phone, body language is missing, so tone of voice is all you have. Make certain you are always neutral, friendly, and polite on the phone because most people can hear boredom, condescension, and rudeness in your voice, even if they can't see your face. As I like to say in training classes, "Angry or entitled people can hear you rolling your eyes over the phone whenever they say something you think is ridiculous. They can hear you looking at your watch if they think you believe they are wasting your time. Pay attention to your tone for the entire call."

We all hate it when a customer service person tries to do two or three things while listening to us, even if it's on our behalf. Get permission to put a patron on hold or to multitask during your phone conversation: "Ma'am, I just need a few moments to look that up. Would you prefer if I called you back or can I put you on a brief hold? I promise to come right back as soon as I have that information. Thanks for your patience." "Sir, it looks like it's going to take me a bit of time to research what you're requesting. I know your time is valuable. I'd feel better calling you back within the hour instead of keeping you on hold. Will that work for you?"

These days, even with our allegedly sophisticated and expensive landline phone systems, there's no absolute guarantee that the person you put on hold will still be there when you come back. And if they're calling on a cell phone, they might just get timed out by the machinery and disconnected, so get a callback number.

The public's confidence in government at any level is as low as ever recorded. Patrons either have unrealistic expectations about what you can do for them or are distrustful of government agencies in general and don't expect much. I always suggest that one way to surprise patrons with a level of unexpected service is to "underpromise and overperform" for them. This means that if you promised them the information by tomorrow, call them back with it today. If you said that you'd have it for them after lunch, get it to them before lunch. They may not immediately recognize the gesture, but it can go a long way toward changing their perception of what libraries and public servants can do for them.

Last, recall the value of setting boundaries over the telephone for a patron's bad behavior. You did not sign on to be yelled at, cursed at, belittled, insulted, or threatened. Give one fair warning, and if the behavior continues and you feel the need to hang up, then hang up. Document the conversation for your supervisor and protect your reputation as a firm, fair, consistent, and assertive library customer service professional.

Dr. Karl Albrecht's Seven Service Sins

My dad has many claims to fame, but his most successful book, of the dozens he has written, was *Service America! Doing Business in the New Economy* (Irwin, 1985), which sold nearly one million copies. In that book, he said that good customer service doesn't happen by accident; it's a managed event, using the right people, systems, and strategies for the business. What follows are the signs he sees in employees who have lost their human touch with their customers. Library supervisors should keep their eyes open for these sins and address them with coaching meetings, using examples if they are exhibited by employees. Too many of these can lead to a rise in the number of valid complaints from patrons about how they are treated.

1. Apathy
2. The Brush-Off
3. Coldness
4. Condescension
5. Robotism
6. The Rule Book
7. The Runaround

From this list, the sin that drives patrons the most crazy, that leads to the most angry complaint calls or visits to supervisors or the library director, and that makes patrons feel like they are being spoken to or treated like a child is the fourth one, condescension. This one can come on when employees are physically and mentally tired at the end of the workday, when they've worked too many days in a row without a break from a sea of demanding patrons, or when they are starting to feel the symptoms of job burnout.

Condescension shows up mostly in an employee's tone and body language: "Yes? What is it this time, sir?" or "You didn't fill out the form correctly now did you, ma'am?" It's critically important to catch yourself before you let condescension "leak out" over the phone or face-to-face. And as a supervisor (or if you want to be one someday), you need to watch for this sin, catch it early, and correct it with examples, support, and coaching meetings. The biggest negative impact of this sin is that patrons go away mad from the encounter with the employee and they don't really know why. It all starts and ends with how they are treated.

Dr. Karl Albrecht's Code of Quality Service

I've annotated the following ten behaviors to match the service rigors in the library world:

1. **Greet each patron immediately or when passing by.** If you're not initially helping them, catch the eye of patrons as you pass. You're onstage all the time on the public floor, and they see you as a representative of the library.

2. **Give each patron you meet your complete attention.** It's easy to get into multitask mode and stay there during an exchange with a patron. It's certainly acceptable to look up things on your computer or in a book; just be careful that you don't get distracted while a patron is asking you questions while you try to do ten things at once.

3. **Make the first thirty seconds count for the patron.** First impressions do count.

4. **Play your part to be real, not phony or bored.** As my dad would say, "You're not allowed to be a Bozo or a Bored Zombie." See your encounters with patrons as your ongoing opportunity to add value, solve problems, and be the information professional that you have trained to become. This attitude of wanting to help people is not about being subservient or sacrificing your personality; it's about feeling good about yourself while you help others.

5. **Show your energy with sincere friendliness.** Never forget that you're onstage. You may have to "act" enthusiastically even when you're tired. Play your part in the play.

6. **Be the patron's problem solver.** You may not be in charge of everything, but you still have the ability to create positive outcomes for patrons, by taking ownership of their issues and finding unique, clever, or outside-the-box solutions for them. Saying, "Let me work on it for a bit and get back to you" is so much stronger than saying, "That's not my job" or "I'm not allowed to do that."

7. **Use your common sense.** I recall a company that asked its employees to try to answer their telephones after the second ring. Some employees would pick it up on the second ring

and then hang it back up again because "No one told us we have to actually speak to anyone, just answer it by the second ring." Your employers are paying you to be smart; prove them right.

8. **Bend the rules when the situation calls for it.** An example: Let's assume that library policy says a patron can't check out any more books if he or she owes at least $10 in fines. One library employee might simply tell the offending patron wanting to check out a book, "Sorry, no can do. Rules are rules. I don't make 'em; I just enforce 'em." A service-oriented library employee would ask the patron, "The computer tells me you owe ten dollars, and you say you only have five dollars on you today? Let's apply that five dollars so you can check out the books you want. We'll get the rest on your next visit." The first employee is certainly correct and following the letter of the law. The second employee is following the spirit of the law and creating a better experience for the patron at the same time. Don't give away the keys to the building, but look for opportunities to bend the rules and still keep your boss and the patron happy.

9. **Make the last thirty seconds count for the patron.** Last impressions count too. Most people remember the beginning of a service encounter and the end of it.

10. **Take good care of yourself.** Service jobs with high human contact can be tiring. You can't be your best if you don't feel your best. Get enough sleep, eat a healthy diet, get some exercise, and don't ever come to work with a bad case of "tequila flu." (All things in moderation.)

Posting and Enforcing Codes of Conduct

I say this with love in my heart, but after having looked at dozens and dozens of code of conduct rules from libraries across the nation, my conclusion is that many of them look and sound like they were written by city attorneys or county counsels, not by true library people. The language often sounds stilted, stiff, and almost biblical (i.e., "Thou shalt not consume thy foods in said building"). This is hardly new news since much about compliance with policies, especially in government, is derived from advice from our legal friends. I like a visible, posted, and patron-friendly code of conduct, written so there are not a lot of gray areas about what you can and can't do, but not sounding so legalistic that patrons get a little mad by the time they're done reading it.

I'm always puzzled when library directors or their employees tell me they have a lot of behavioral problems in their libraries and yet the only place to find the code of conduct is on a clipboard behind the circulation desk (which no patron has ever actually asked to read) or on the library's website.

Having your code of conduct posted in several highly visible places throughout your library is an important first step toward getting patrons to be compliant and keeping them that way. Hiding these important rules from view is a mistake because it allows patrons to fall back on standard answers about noncompliance: "No one ever told me." "I didn't know I couldn't do or say that." "You're picking on me because I'm [fill in the blank]." "Other people are doing the same thing." "I've been coming here for a long time, and I always thought I could do this or that." And on and on.

I'm a big believer in putting the rules of library conduct on large posters that are visible near the entrances and other common areas (so you can see them from outer space). I also like changing the language from negative to positive; for example, "No cell phone calls in the library" should be rewritten as "Please take your cell phone calls outside," or "No eating or drinking in the library" can be recast as "Please enjoy your food and beverages before you come inside." You will get better compliance from patrons and create more of an "Enjoy our library" tone by using positive language rather than negative rules, which suggest, "This is how we run our library, like a bureaucracy."

In the forthcoming two chapters on typical challenging patron behaviors and common challenging patron types, I'll address both the language for codes of conduct and how to respond in different ways that can help you sound more human and less lawyerly, approaches that tend to get you better results.

CHAPTER 3

Challenging Patron Behaviors

In my workshops, this question arises early: "When is the best time to confront certain patron behaviors that are either violating our policies or our code of conduct?" The answer is not that complex: When the patron's behavior hurts the business of the library and affects the way other patrons use the library or when it impacts library staff in a negative way, then you have to address it.

As an example, when you see something you know is against your policy or code of conduct—a homeless person is passed out and snoring away in one of the chairs in the back of the stacks—ask yourself, "Is this person hurting our business?" If the answer is no, then move on to your other duties. But if the person's behavior does bother other patrons, then address it by approaching Sleeping Beauty and saying in a tone loud enough to rouse him, "Sir? Are you okay? Are you sick or do you need medical care?" When he mumbles that he's not sick and doesn't need an ambulance, express your relief that he's fine and then gently tell him he can't sleep in the library.

This creative approach demands that you think a bit outside the box, but it accomplishes several things: It demonstrates empathy—maybe the guy really is sick and does need paramedics—and it solves the problem in a low-key way, without starting an argument about his God-given or constitutional right to sleep where he wants to sleep.

A light touch is always preferable in the beginning because you can always get tougher if you need to. It's difficult to start out as a strict disciplinarian and then be able to back it down to Mr. or Ms. Friendly Staffer because you've already set the tone as tough. Start friendly, even with a little bit of humor, and if that doesn't work, you can always put a sterner edge to your voice. Let's look at two common patron issues as examples of this "try a lighter touch first" approach: Eating and cell phones.

A guy is eating a greasy roast beef sandwich at one of your tables. He has his food spread out in front of him: Pickles, fries, coleslaw, soda—the works. The "old you" might come over and start giving him the what-for: "Sir, you aren't allowed to eat in the library! It's against our policy. Other people have to use this area and your leftover food can draw ants, and furthermore…." Let's try a different, lighter approach, using the "new you": "Hi, sir. How are you today? Sorry to interrupt your lunch. Is that roast beef? Is that spicy mustard on there? I love those big deli pickles. I wish I could join you, but, and I know you probably just forgot this, you can't eat in the library. Do you want me to save your spot here at this table while you finish up outside?"

A woman is gabbing on her cell phone while sitting at a table with her laptop. You can hear her across the room (as can people in the next ZIP code). She exhibits the usual lack of social intelligence by people who don't seem to realize that most every other person on the planet has a cell phone, cell phones aren't novel or new anymore, and no one wants to hear any part of their conversations. Old you: "Ma'am, you cannot use your cell phone in the library. It's against our policy. You'll just have to take that call outside. Other people are trying to read or study and your call is disrupting their ability to…." New you: You make the universal hand and face gestures to get her to stop talking and say, "Hi, ma'am. It looks like you're having an important personal or business call there. The cell coverage in this room is not very good, which is why we don't allow cell phone calls in the library. Do you want me to save your spot here and watch your laptop and purse for a few minutes while you finish your call outside?" Here's another variation of this same theme: "If you want to walk over to that unused technology room over there, I'll watch your stuff while you finish your call. We don't usually let people in there, but I know you'll just be a few minutes."

For Sandwich Guy, you're just trying to get him to cooperate without causing a scene, so you use a little humor about mustard and pickles. The message is the same in both scenarios—you can't eat in the library—but your response in the second version is more humane while still getting to the same conclusion. For Cell Phone Lady, you are politely interrupting her but giving her a face-saving way to take the call in another location while you watch her stuff (note the time limit you put on her to get back in a few minutes). You achieve the same desired outcome using both approaches, just with a lighter touch in the second one that also plays a bit to her ego of being such a Very Important Person.

Most people want to cooperate and want to follow the rules, but they hate being told what to do, especially by people younger than they are, and particularly if what you say includes even a hint of a parental or condescending tone.

The Twenty Most Challenging Library Behavior Problems

The following discussion about some of the most common behavioral issues in libraries should raise some questions for you: Are these issues that you regularly or rarely face? Do you have written policies about these concerns or are they something you address more informally? Are these issues covered in your posted code of conduct? Which of these twenty behavior problems hurt your business the most, take up the most staff time, or generate the most staff complaints or patron complaints? Do you need to reprioritize your responses to some of these issues?

Smoking in or near the Library

Are patrons allowed to vape in your library, that is, smoke electronic cigarettes? Do you ever see evidence of patrons smoking in your restrooms or in more secluded areas of your facility? In states like Colorado and Washington that have legalized marijuana use, do you ever see evidence of pot use inside or outside your facilities? Is the mess created by the remnants of smokeless tobacco an issue in your library? Do you find matches or lighters in your facility or any tobacco products in designated children's areas?

Soliciting/Panhandling in or near the Library

It seems like there is a homeless person at all four traffic islands at every four-way intersection in this country, all of them carrying the same cardboard signs asking for money. Most people are tolerant of this approach but despise aggressive panhandling, especially in public access points where they are trying to come and go. Does your code of conduct address panhandling in the library? Is this problem rare or common in your facility? How is the police response to this issue? If it's not already in place, can you get support from your city attorney or county counsel to create a municipal code or ordinance banning panhandling at the library? Do your city or county homeless advocacy groups have a "same as cash/take a token" program, instead of having people give the homeless money? (The site GiveTokens. org offers a great example of safe support of the homeless.) Are you able to ask the homeless who engage in this practice to stop and they mostly comply, or have you lost control of the problem?

Threats or Assaults on Staff or Patrons

With regards to staff, Cardinal Safety and Security Rule #1 should be this: "We will call the police for any person who physically assaults a staff member. That staff member will have the right to request a police report and make a citizen's arrest. We will create our own Security Incident Report as well." Anything less than full adoption of this rule and staff will feel unprotected, unappreciated, and vulnerable. If there are no consequences for patrons who hit staff members, the message sent to both parties is that such behavior is somehow acceptable.

Cardinal Safety and Security Rule #2: "We will ask a patron who has been assaulted by any other patron if he or she wants us to call the police to make a report. If one or more of our employees saw the act, they will serve as witnesses for both the police report and our own Security Incident Report."

Cardinal Safety and Security Rule #3: In states that have penal code sections covering people who make threats, "We will ask staff or patrons if they want to make a police report for any threats to harm them by another patron that would put a reasonable person in fear for his or her safety. We will create our own Security Incident Report."

In the wake of so many workplace violence and school violence threats that were verbalized (including bomb threats), many states have created so-called "terroristic threats" or "menacing statutes" that make threatening words illegal. As an example, in California, the Penal Code Section 422 criminal threats statute can be prosecuted as a felony under certain circumstances.

I'm aware that a police report is not a bulletproof shield in these cases, but the value of making such a report outweighs not doing anything. The person who made the threats will have a record of doing so in police computers; there is often a follow-up by officers or detectives in these cases, during which they confront the threatener as to the reasons and meanings of his or her threats and warn them to stop; and these cases do get prosecuted. There are people in county jails and state prisons for merely using their words and not the gun or bomb that they said they had.

Intimidating Staff or Patrons

There are male and female bullies everywhere, including the library, sad to say. They have made their way in the world by throwing their weight around, literally and figuratively. The bad news is that this approach often works for them because service people on the receiving end are often intimidated, embarrassed, and even fearful of telling them no. It takes courage as a library supervisor or employee to stand up to these patrons when they try to strong-arm you into not paying fines, checking out too much material, or violating your rules or code of conduct. The good news is that it's still your library and you have the right and the obligation to operate it in a way that's good for all patrons (and staff), not just for people who raise their voices or pitch a fit and fall in it. Stick to your guns, don't back down, get help from colleagues, change the ratios of confrontation by getting more help from a coworker or staff member, and be firm, fair, consistent, and assertive with those patrons who try to bully you.

Not Following Library Rules

The library is neither a prison camp nor a gypsy camp. We have rules in place so people can enjoy the facility, but we shouldn't lose our humanity in the process. Little kids run in libraries and climb on the furniture. Little old ladies and little old men like to have long conversations with staff, even when it's busy. Teenagers spend hours on their hair, makeup, or clothing so they can strut around and impress one another at the library. Some people in the library are too self-important to realize their impact on other people. Some people in the library are wonderfully or painfully eccentric. You should already know the difference between the spirit of the law and the letter of the law. If a patron's behavior hurts the business of the library, meaning that it impacts the safe and fair use of the facility, then enforce your policies or code of conduct. If it doesn't, then save your energy for when it does. No one can accuse you of playing favorites or overstepping boundaries or not doing your job when you are always firm, fair, consistent, and assertive.

Violating Temporary Restraining Orders

Having worked as a domestic violence investigator, I've often questioned the efficacy of TROs. They work really well for good rule followers, but, unfortunately, many of the people who are served with them have already demonstrated they cannot follow the rules. I'll talk a bit more in Chapter 4 about domestic violence–related TROs, which may come to your library from a staff member or a patron. For this section, let's stick to TROs or stay-away orders that we've placed on patrons, probably because of their long history of obnoxious behavior in the library or because they have assaulted staff or other patrons. I have talked to library staff about restrained parties and with patrons who have been kicked out. A lot of the restrained people I have seen or heard about are mentally ill or homeless or both. They are often under a verbal TRO, whereby they have agreed to stay out of the library for a solid thirty days. I find it fascinating how effective this no-legal-papers method is with this population. Some of them actually remind the library director or library staff on their way into work each day: "Hi, Ms. Jones! Only nineteen more days until I can come back in!" They will say this in a hopeful, positive way, which suggests to me that they have indeed learned their lesson about following the rules, and I point to this as an example of how the impact of consequences can work.

For actual TROs against chronically aggressive people, make your decision as soon as they are served to call the police and report a violation every single time they violate the order by showing up, calling, or making contact with staff or the facility. The cops are going to get tired of coming out to write the same report, and they will look for ways to expedite this person's trip to jail for the violation and for being in contempt of the judge's order. Now is not the time to get wishy-washy about this person's impact or intentions. Don't minimize the contact: "He only came inside once, but he didn't bother anyone." Stay away means stay away, and the police need to come to the scene to make an arrest, if he or she is still on-site, or take a report, if he or she has left. (When I teach patrol theory on this issue to officers, I remind them that the suspect is probably watching their arrival from a distance and that they should look to grab him or her while they are en route to the location.)

I address a related issue, the use of so-called "cease and desist" letters, in the final section of this chapter. These letters are often sent by a library director or city attorney or county counsel to people who make threats inside libraries or, more likely, through e-mails, letters, faxes, or phone calls.

Sexual Behaviors against Staff or Patrons

Cardinal Safety and Security Rule #1, discussed earlier in relation to people who physically assault staff or patrons, applies as well to illegal sexual behaviors by patrons. We should call the police and begin the reporting process. At no time should we ever try to discourage staff members or patrons from making a police report if they want one, even when we think the suspect is too old, too young, mentally ill, or developmentally disabled and cannot or should not be held accountable. No free passes on these behaviors.

Trespassing in Restricted or Employees-Only Areas

The most important question about this behavior is this: Is it accidental or intentional? I've been lost inside many libraries because the signage is not great. (Think like a patron, wander around your facility, and see if it's easy to get lost because you need more or better signs.) Some patrons are caught up in their own world and show up in the employee break room because they can't read signs or weren't paying attention. If it happens more than once, I'm thinking that person is a potential thief. Smart crooks know that female employees generally put their purses in the file drawers of their desks or under their desks, and that male employees usually leave their backpacks or bags near or on their desks. If staff members are busy, a smart thief can get into the back room and be gone with personal items, cell phones, tablets, and the like in a few minutes.

I'm a fan of "Employees Only" signs on doors that are also locked or key card controlled. Too many library employees trade security for convenience, saying, "We put this chain across the hallway that says 'Employees Only'" or "I come and go through the staff door all day long. It's a hassle to keep using my key to unlock it." Too bad. We need to do a better job of keeping patrons or crooks on their side of our doors. Consider that the security device of choice in many libraries is that little swinging gate on the circulation desk that separates the patron side from the employee side (you know the one; it has that complicated latch which never works correctly). We have the right and obligation to keep employees safe by keeping their side of the building secured.

Bringing Bikes, Skates, and Skateboards into the Library

This is a "Let's test their boundaries" issue in many libraries, especially with teenagers and used-to-be teenagers. Use the model "Introduce. Explain. Ask.": "Hi, I'm Steve from the library. I see you brought your bike inside. Because of our insurance regulations, we're not allowed to let folks bring their bikes inside. Maybe you forgot your lock today or the bike rack was full? Could I ask you to leave it outside before you come back in? Thanks for your help."

The police in a lot of cities spend their time chasing skateboarders out of parking structures, city halls, parks, and anyplace with lots of concrete edges or railings. If skateboarders (and their BMX bike-riding brethren) are doing damage to the outside of your facility, talk to your facilities, maintenance, or public works staff for help with deterrent devices.

Theft or Vandalism of Library Materials or Equipment or Staff Members' or Patrons' Personal Property

A friend of mine used to be the director of loss prevention for a big-box mall department store. He would watch a shoplifter put an item into his or her coat pocket or purse and then he would approach the crook and say, "Hi! I work here at the store and I noticed you just put that watch [scarf, necktie, etc.] into your pocket. I'm sure you are just holding on to it so you can continue to shop. If you'll give it to me, I'll take it up to the cashiers and have them hold it for you until you're ready to pay." The would-be thief would hand over the swag and slink away, hopefully never to be seen again.

A similar approach can work in your library. You see a patron stuff a book or a DVD into his or her backpack. As the patron leaves, catch him or her at the door and say, "Hi! I work here and I noticed that you put a book or a DVD in your bag there. Why don't you give it to me so I can take it up to the circulation desk and have them hold it for you until you're ready to use your card to check it out."

Theft controls in libraries tend to be connected to the culture of the facility. Some libraries have a "don't confront, don't chase" policy for any patron who steals. Others ask their security officers to have a conversation similar to the one just described. Other libraries ask staff to be vigilant and to address the issue of proven thefts (ones they witnessed) with patrons by asking them to return the materials. I think we have to find a happy medium between letting anyone walk out with whatever he or she wants—because the alarm gates are turned off or always broken—and tackling a nice little old lady in the parking lot because she accidentally put an extra book in her canvas bag. Again, we're back to a firm, fair, consistent, and assertive response to real thieves that sends the message, in the library and on the streets, that it's not allowed, okay, or easy to steal from the library.

Any proven or witnessed theft of expensive library property should prompt a call to the police. I once saw a security camera video of a woman who walked out with a flat-screen television between her legs, covered by a long skirt and taking many, many, very, very small steps to the parking lot. (Where there's a will—and there's always a will—there's a way.) Any theft of library tablets, computers, phones, laptops, projectors, televisions, or other expensive stuff warrants a police report.

Staff members or patrons should always be given the option of calling the police and making a theft report in those situations where you've caught the thief and he or she tried to give back the items "no questions asked." Police report or not, you need to create a Security Incident Report for the library, same as for incidents of vandalism.

Misusing Restrooms

The list of possible behaviors inside these walls is too uncomfortable to contemplate. In my Perfect Library World, you would have a courageous and vigilant security guard who would make regular rounds through the facility, including sporadic checks in the restrooms, to ensure there is no damage, sink showering, smoking, or sexual behavior going on.

No Shoes/No Shirt/No Pants?

I'm not a lawyer, so I'm not certain you can force people to wear clothes inside the library, unless you have a specific municipal code about it. You can certainly put "Please wear your shoes and shirts while enjoying our library" in your code of conduct and try to enforce that as best you can. Some people are very free with their bodies, which is not always the best thing for the rest of us to see.

Abandoning or Not Attending to Children

I rant in some detail in Chapter 4 about the need to call the police if you suspect that an alleged parent has dropped off a child at the library and told him or her to spend the next twelve hours there alone. This is child abuse, and you are not in the business of babysitting at-risk kids, all day and into the evening, as part of your work duties. For little kids who are left alone to wander the library while their inattentive parents read, doze, or gab away on their cell phones, you might try this approach: "Hi, sir [or ma'am]. I've noticed that your son [or daughter] has wandered out of your sight. As a parent myself, I'm always worried that my child is going to come across another person who might want to hurt my baby. I know you don't want that to happen to your little angel, right? We can't always guarantee what kind of strangers come into the library, those who have no intention of getting a book. Do you understand what I mean? Thanks for making me feel better about your taking good care of your child when he [or she] is here."

Bringing in Comfort Animals versus Service Animals

I discuss this emerging civil and emotional rights issue at length in Chapter 4. I fear for the future of this whole subject, as it devolves into lawsuits and accusations that people who work in libraries don't care about the emotional well-being of their patrons. We do; we just don't want to spend our working hours looking for their missing "comfort boa constrictor" or wandering "emotional support goat."

Since I'm told it's apparently fairly easy to complete an online questionnaire and pay a fee to get your beast of choice listed as a card-carrying, certified "emotional support animal," I am concerned that people will want to bring their untrained, amateur service dogs into the library and then cause a barking and growling confrontation with staff or other patrons. As the owner of seven dogs (don't ask), I think I know a bit about canine behaviors. Thus, in the interest of staff and patron safety around untrained dogs coming into the library, here are a few key points:

- **Know the difference between barking dogs and growling dogs.** Barking dogs are generally fearful and are trying to draw attention to their situation. Growling dogs are not fearful; they are preparing to bite someone.
- **Make careful eye contact with dogs.** Dogs read the eyes of people and other dogs constantly. Look slightly to the side and don't make direct eye contact with the dog until you're sure it's friendly. Dogs operate with their noses like we use our eyes, so

let them sniff the back of your hand before you get any closer to them.

- **Use strong and assertive verbal commands, and even shout if you have to, to get the dog's attention.** As the Dog Whisperer Cesar Millan would suggest, you have to break the dogs' chain of concentration on their own negative energy before they will listen or pay attention to you. For any vicious dogs, get help from your city or county animal control officers, law enforcement, or the uniformed division of the ASPCA.

Sleeping

This is a gray area. I've nodded off in libraries before (I suspect the publishers of certain thick textbooks of putting some type of anesthetic in their inks). I once witnessed a library staff member come across a homeless guy who had stripped himself naked, climbed up on a table, covered himself with a recent issue of *The New York Times*, and fallen asleep, approach the man and say, "Well, he's kind of reading it, I guess." My advice is always to ask yourself this: What is the impact on the business? Is the guy snoring and bothering other people, or is he tucked into a corner of the facility and no one sees him but staff? Is he sleeping off a drunk and therefore will wake up like a bear with a sore rear, or is it a college kid cramming for finals who has crashed from not enough caffeine?

If you do decide to wake someone, never touch the person; use your voice commands only. Many people, and most of all the homeless, who are used to being attacked or mugged while they sleep, don't like being startled awake.

Bringing in Prohibited or Contraband Items

Such items include firearms, ammunition, fireworks, knives or obvious weapons, drugs, or child pornography. You aren't searching people, so the best you can do is post the information as part of your code of conduct and have staff pay attention to what they see people hauling around. There has been a significant shift in this country in many states to allowing people with valid Carrying a Concealed Weapon (CCW) permits to bring their guns into most government buildings, including libraries. Of course, government buildings like courthouses, jails, mental health facilities, and city council chambers or county boardrooms generally still don't allow concealed firearms to be brought into their facilities, so there you go. I have seen some libraries post "No Firearms Allowed in the Library" signs that include even those people who have a CCW permit, but how do we really know whether they are carrying a gun or not? It's no small matter to consider that some patrons you talk to may be armed or have a gun in their belongings, whether or not they have a CCW permit.

Blocking the Aisles

If you have a problem with homeless people in your library, you've seen this same song, different verse, each day: Using their bodies like Sherpas or your carts, they come in piled high with their personal belongings, sneaking shopping carts or wagons into your facility and carrying bags and bags and bags of their collected items, often mixed with recyclables and other trash. The usual rule applies: Be firm, fair, consistent, and assertive, and set standards as to how much is enough and how much is too much. Use my favorite admonishment: "You can't bring all that stuff in here if you want to stay here. You can be here, but all that stuff cannot. I'm asking you to make a choice." Many times, this face-saving way out works, largely because they know they can't risk leaving their bags outside, so they leave with them.

Eating and Drinking

Patrons should have no food and drinks in the library unless you specifically allow it. Some libraries have become full-fledged coffee shops and cafés; others don't even allow bottles of water. Follow your code of conduct.

Using Cell Phones

Note my earlier suggestions under Not Following Library Rules for a lighter touch here. We've long passed the point at which people even care that they are being offensive with their cell phones. Do the best you can to enforce some quiet time in your library.

Misusing the Computers, Printers, Copiers, Internet, or Wi-Fi

This can take unique forms, like downloading child pornography or trying to introduce viruses into your systems with thumb drives. You need a written information technology (IT) policy (borrow the language from good policies at other libraries); posted signage near your computers, printers, and copiers about inappropriate usages; and stiff firewall protections from your city or county IT providers.

Many years ago, I heard the following story and it warmed what's left of my jaded, old-cop heart. A man came to the library on a regular basis to use the Internet for the purposes of downloading and then printing out color porn photos on the color printer kept behind the circulation desk. He would come to the library, log on, download his porn photos of choice, send them to the color printer, pay for his pages, and leave. This went on for weeks and months. Finally, the little old lady librarian (always my favorite kind) working behind the desk and collecting his photos and money had reached the end of her rope. (Imagine this is your saintly grandma here, to get the maximum value from this story.) She got on the library's public address system and said, "Will the man who printed out the penis pictures please come pick them up?" He came slinking over, paid for his photos, left the building, and never returned. If I ever meet her, I will hug her.

The Futility of Cease-and-Desist Letters in Threat Cases

Threat assessment work around difficult customers, taxpayers, or library patrons demands creativity, patience, intuition, and the ability not only to think outside the box but also to help (or urge) others to do so as well. One area where I run into difficulties is during discussions, often with city or county attorneys, about the need to send a threatener, who has contacted a library by e-mail, letter, or phone call, a cease-and-desist letter. This person may be a former employee who quit in anger or was terminated in a less than positive way, an unpaid vendor, or an embattled patron. Such people often choose to target the library with a barrage of e-mails or calls, designed to disrupt operations and make staff members fear for their lives. In these cases, senior library management wants answers and turns to HR, law enforcement, the city attorney or county counsel, and me to take action.

In my experience, e-mail threats are much less of a security concern than are unannounced visits by former employees or angry patrons. Threatening from a distance is a different mind-set from screaming in the library at a frightened staffer. This is at the heart of the matter; some people use threatening e-mails, texts, or written letters (less likely these days) or menacing voice messages left on their target's business or personal voice mail. Their use of electronic distance is intentional. Their thinking goes, "I can reach out to threaten you anytime and from anywhere, just by pressing a few buttons. And there is nothing you can do to stop me."

Would I rather work on a threat case where the perpetrator sent an ominous e-mail from IHateYourGuts@yahoo.com or the same e-mail from MyFirstName.MyLastName@yahoo.com? The first threatener is using an anonymous e-mail address to do just that—remain anonymous. This person fears the consequences, wants to continue to play cat-and-mouse, and may think that shuffling through a series of fake e-mail addresses makes it harder for him or her to be tracked or identified. The second threatener uses his or her name and self-identifies, so there is no intent to hide. This person is saying, to a current or former supervisor, coworker, HR, the police, or the library in general, "Yeah, it's me. So now what are you going to do about it?"

The behavior of self-identified threateners is more of a concern because they are not being covert, but instead overt, in their threats of harm. Many electronic threateners perceive what they're doing as not necessarily illegal (which it is in most states), and they enjoy being provocative, all-powerful, and disruptive. You certainly should be more concerned when ex-employees, domestic violence partners of current employees, angry vendors or patrons, or mentally ill strangers enter your library facilities with no warning. The electronic threatener gives you advance notice and a great evidentiary paper trail of dates, times, and words. The phone threatener gives you evidence of tone, malice, and threatening statements, which you can take to the police for a possible arrest or to a judge should we decide to get a civil protection order.

This is where the paradoxical part of your work comes into play. As the US Secret Service has reported as part of its 1998 Exceptional Case Study Project, some people *make* threats and some people *pose* threats. We often have more to be concerned about from people who pose threats than from those who make them. Overt threats mean something different from covert threats. As such, we need to handle these cases in completely different ways, and this can take some hard convincing to get the city or county stakeholders to agree. Sometimes simply observing the stream of messages is an effective course of action. We can watch for signs of depression, bipolar disorder, loss of hope, statements about weapons possession, or suicidal or homicidal ideations. But senior leadership and the attorneys, who may not understand the threat assessment process, demand actions, not observations.

After the usual plethora of threatening calls or e-mails has scared enough people in the library, the city attorney or county counsel will often craft a strongly worded cease-and-desist e-mail or written letter to send to the perpetrator. The language often includes statements like this: "If you do not immediately cease all contact with our library, via any electronic means, we will be forced to take direct legal action against you." In theory, this could include getting a TRO, calling the police to make a criminal threats or harassment case report, working with the telephone provider to trap or block calls, filing a civil suit for damages, or having the person arrested. In operation, these good ideas rarely happen. When the threatener makes another call, sends another letter, or posts yet another e-mail, the library's response is to send yet another cease-and-desist letter, with even more "strong language" in it. The threatener continues, the lawyers continue, and the cycle continues.

You may hear counsel say that the reason for the cease-and-desist letter process is to "have something in the file" to show a judge or to demonstrate due diligence to frightened employees or senior management. In reality, these letters only encourage the threatener to keep playing by hitting the ball back across the net with every new letter. The solution is clear: If it's deemed necessary, send the first (and only) cease-and-desist letter to the subject, and if he or she violates the conditions, then follow up with the enforcing actions promised in the letter. Break the cycle by not creating it.

If our goal in threat assessment is to gather as much information as possible to make good decisions about our response, then why not analyze every message the threatener sends, by whatever means it comes in? We can ask the IT experts for the city or county to redirect the sender's e-mails to our attention, change the target employee's phone number and continue to collect and assess the subject's voice mails, or collect any mail correspondence before it reaches the target employee. We can and should minimize the electronic threatener's impact but still continue to collect the messages. Cease-and-desist letters without consequences are useless and give the power of disruption back to the threatener.

A case in point: Many years ago, I received a copy of both sides of an envelope sent to a library on the West Coast by a patron who was clearly mentally ill. (This was in the days before e-mail became the primary way to communicate.) The front and back of the patron's envelope were completely covered in hearts with arrows through them, random dates, squiggles, and other doodles. Both sides also featured some cryptic messages about the death of someone who was supposedly murdered in the 1960s, and inside was a rambling letter about missing library materials the sender said he had returned. A manager at the library, perhaps at the request of his boss, sent a foreshadowed cease-and-desist letter to the patron in which he made the understandable mistake of saying, "I am returning your recent mailing. I do not understand why you are sending me these things."

As you can probably guess, for the patron—who I suspect was schizophrenic—it was now "Game On." The next package to the library, which he sent to other library employees as well, was the patron's seven-page rambling letter, I'm told, plus a collection of random news articles and thirty-eight pages of photocopies of pictures from old *Playboy* magazines. The patron's muddled thinking in this situation probably went this way: "I got a response from the library, but they're confused as to the intent of my message. I need to explain myself in far greater detail and right away!"

This led to another letter—this time from the library director—using the more recognizable cease-and-desist language: "You must cease mailing these materials to the library manager or to any other staff member at the public library. If you continue to do so, I will seek legal recourse." I never heard the end of the story, but if I had to guess, I'd say the cycle continued, with letters going to the patron telling him to stop and packages coming back to the library with even more detail as to why he just couldn't, until everyone there knew about every detail of his plans and schemes.

As Gavin de Becker, celebrity security expert and author of the best-selling book on intuition, *The Gift of Fear: Survival Signals That Protect Us from Violence*, likes to say, "Sometimes, when you engage, you enrage." In other words, if you get letters or e-mails from patrons who ramble and rant but don't suggest they want to come in and do something illegal, like bomb the building, shoot the staff, or kill the President, if you don't let them check out a certain book (or other demand), in which case you need to call the police, then let them ramble and rant.

In those cases, we should observe and monitor their behavior for signs that they are either escalating or have become attracted to a new target and subsequently faded away. Watching and waiting is not a popular strategy because it feels like we need to "do something." Well, we are doing something; we're watching and waiting for signs that the patron is getting worse:

Engaging in boundary probing (showing up at the facility and causing confrontations), bothering staff repeatedly over the phone, or otherwise increasing the frequency of contacts and with more disturbing behaviors, in which case we immediately call the police.

You should save every piece of odd written correspondence that comes to your facility, whether sent by mail to you, e-mailed to you or other staff members, or dropped off at the library. Such correspondence may not always mean that the situation is dangerous, but if it turns that way, you can go to the police with the special file folder you've created just for that person's contacts and ask them to step in to assess and investigate.

You don't have to and you shouldn't necessarily respond to strange messages that come across your desk, but you should at least keep them to see if a pattern develops over time, showing that a certain patron is getting more and more angry, desperate, unsatisfied, threatening, or hostile.

★ CHAPTER 4

Common Types of Challenging Patrons

I n all encounters with the types of people discussed in this chapter, remember these Rules of Engagement:

- Stay firm, fair, consistent, and assertive in the enforcement of your code of conduct or facility use policies.
- Since most people like to vent, let them, while you validate their words with phrases like these: "I see." "I understand." "I can tell you're upset." "I'm sorry that happened; tell me more about what happened before I got here." "You could be right; let me help you by helping me."
- Always remember that people will cooperate if they can do so with their dignity intact, so be as empathetic as you can, even if you have to role-play it.
- Stay out of the face-to-face zone when dealing with angry, irrational, or unpredictable people. Stand slightly at an angle to them and stay about an arm's length away, plus a step.
- Use proxemic barriers like desks, counters, tables, carts, shelves, windows, or doors if you feel the intuitive need to put something between you and the angry person.
- Use the Assertive Whisper and physical movement when you engage with angry people. When you talk quietly instead of trying to match their loud tones, you send a unique subliminal message: "This is a professional workplace here. I will not shout at you, and I will model the tone I'd like you to use with me." Physical movement can help you draw them away from

other patrons so as not to disrupt the library, and it can help
you guide them toward the exit as you walk and talk.

I'm a big fan of the book *Crucial Conversations: Tools for Talking When
Stakes Are High* (McGraw-Hill, 2002), by Kerry Patterson, Joseph Grenny,
Ron McMillan, and Al Switzler, who discuss how to talk about tough topics
with people. They define "crucial conversations" as those where "opinions
vary, the stakes are high, and emotions run strong." Many of the patrons
(and even some library staff) discussed in this chapter have strong ideas
and feelings about the issues at hand; they want to be heard, even if the
patrons know the consequences could be getting kicked out, barred tempo-
rarily or permanently from the library, or getting arrested. As the authors of
Crucial Conversations note, these aren't just *important* conversations, they're
crucial ones.

The following sections, in no particular order, collect all of the patrons
that librarians have told me about over the past fifteen years who have the
highest potential to complicate their days. If I had only three pieces of
advice to give you about having crucial conversations with these folks, they
would be these:

1. **STOP saying "Calm down!" to people who are upset.** This
   has never worked in the history of humanity, and it won't work
   for you. Saying this just makes people angrier (think back to
   when someone has said it to you and how that made you feel
   even more upset).

2. **Be prepared to act the part.** Customer service professionals know they have to fake it once in a while. When you're
   tired, hungry, grouchy, or just want to be left alone, that's the
   time you have to step onto the stage and *act* enthusiastic. Be
   approachable, friendly, neutral in your tone and body language,
   and assertive as you give help to people.

3. **Know your limits.** It's okay to say, "I don't know the answer to
   that question" or "I can't help you with that" and to *set boundaries* about how much time, information, and physical presence
   you must devote to patrons who want to monopolize you.

Angry Patrons

It's no secret that angry people like to vent. Keep in mind that they're mostly angry at the situation, not at you personally. Letting them vent helps in several ways: It allows the person to be heard; it buys you some time to figure out your best response or solution to the issue; it allows time for a colleague or a supervisor to join you, if necessary, to change the ratios of confrontation, watch your back, and help lower the emotional temperature.

The second and most critical step in allowing patrons to vent is to validate their concerns by using semantically supportive statements like these: "I see." "I understand." "You could be right." "I'm sorry that happened to you." "Thanks for telling me about this issue." "Let's see what we can do together to make things right." Allowing them to vent shrinks their big energy balloon and helps you figure out what they need. People like to hear the sound of their own voices, so let them talk. The validation step is critical because it shows empathy and helps the patrons feel heard, listened to, valued, and appreciated. Remember to use your best acting skills, if necessary, so you can send them away relatively satisfied (the best and most realistic service goal across a spectrum of their possible feelings about how they were treated) and thinking that you did your best on their behalf.

Threatening Patrons

Library people will often tell me, "Steve, it's easy for you to stand in front of us and talk about how to deal with threatening people. You look like you're in pretty good shape; you're a weight lifter and were a martial artist. You used to be a cop. You know how to make people do what you say. We get scared of people who threaten us. Don't you get scared?" Of course! Right down to my socks. I don't like dealing with threatening people any more than you do, and I've been plenty afraid for my safety in certain high-risk situations in which I saw that my words were not working.

But physical size isn't the primary factor behind success when dealing with scary people. It's more about attitude—bravado, if you will. I once saw a large and angry homeless guy cause a scene in the library that scared staff members. A little old lady librarian (as I've mentioned before, always my favorite kind) marched up to him and said, "Young man, you can't say those things here. You'll have to leave—now." He said, "Uh, yes, ma'am," gathered up his things, and slunk out of the building. If I had tried that with him, he probably would've wanted to fight me.

And remember our discussion of *alignment* in Chapter 2 on customer service? Certain staff members align more effectively with angry or threatening patrons, based on age, race, gender, or previous contacts. If you have better rapport with a person than your colleague does, take over. It's possible for some situations to start with the patron being angry and then escalating into threats, but it's also possible to start with a threatening patron who can be deescalated to being relatively reasonable. Review the next chapter's discussion of the unique threat assessment concept called "Hunters versus Howlers" so you'll know which one you have in front of you. For threatening patrons, you have to decide what kind of consequences to enforce, including asking them to leave or calling the police.

Entitled Patrons

These tend to be your classic scene makers. They raise their voices to be heard by other people so they can feel important and let you know they're feeling superior. Take this in stride. They do this everywhere they go, including the bank, the restaurant, and the grocery store. Many of these people are vigorously unhappy in their lives, and they take it out on the people around them. Put aside your tendency to want to defend yourself or argue with them.

Don't match their tone. Use the Assertive Whisper: The louder they get, the quieter you get. Stand your ground and don't let them belittle you. Sometimes it helps to get a supervisor to take over the situation, not because you can't handle it, but because these people want to talk to an authority figure, which is how they see themselves. Your boss should say the exact same thing you just said, word for word, and usually the patrons will accept it because they believe they are speaking to an equal. Don't take it personally; it's just business.

Eccentric or Needy Patrons

These patrons can be time monopolizers. They may live odd, lonely, or even desperate lives, and they see the library as a refuge, a place to be, and a place to get human contact. They aren't usually threatening or dangerous, but they can try your patience. So take your Patience Pills when you see them coming and treat them with the dignity they deserve. Another problem with such patrons is that they either won't take no for answer or will tell you that your proposed solutions won't work. You can end up in a verbal tennis match, sending yet another possible solution back and forth over the net, until you're exhausted. They like playing verbal tennis, so you have to use Albrecht's Rule of Three Answers: Set your limit at three possible solutions and stick to it. Keep repeating those three options until they either get it or you have to end the conversation. If they say, "Those things won't work for me; you don't know your job very well," you can say, "You could be right, but I have to get back to work."

Vandals

Vandalism is a crime of stealth. If you can make frequent eye contact with those patrons who you suspect may have a scratch awl, marker, or can of spray paint in their backpacks, then you can give off the message, "I'm watching you," which may send them to other locations. Scratchers, taggers, and gangsters all like to leave their marks on your books, shelves, carts, interior or exterior walls, bathrooms, mirrors, windows, and even the toilet seats. You won't ever stop this behavior, but you can control it by removing or replacing the tagged materials or having someone from your facilities staff paint over or repair the fixtures as soon as you can schedule the work. Tagging and scratching left unfixed beget more tagging and scratching. In their world, if they see the marks of another crew, they will cross them out and put their marks over top. Pull materials, paint over the offending marks, and do the best you can to keep the restrooms and other common areas clean from their attacks. This takes vigilance, but it's necessary. Call the police and report large-scale or expensive damage. The cops often recognize these marks and can make arrests, and the prosecutors can ask the judge to demand restitution back to your facility.

Gang Members

This group values respect more than oxygen, water, or food. Gang members are hypersensitive to being slighted, which is often why they shoot their rivals for looking at them the wrong way. You don't need to kiss their backsides, but you do have to be careful not to embarrass or disrespect them, especially in front of their pals or girlfriends. Not every kid or adult who sags his pants, wears his hat crooked, or has a lot of tattoos is a gang member. But you will often get a vibe from certain guys who seem as if they may have been in state prison as recently as that morning.

Treat these people politely, assertively, and fairly and you will usually not have problems with them. If they feel you have disrespected or embarrassed them, then their response could become problematic. They have long memories. Gang members use the library for a variety of both normal and illegitimate reasons: They recruit new members, intimidate people they know, sell drugs, and tag or mark library materials with their gang names, colors, or signs, or sometimes they simply need a book to do their homework (many of them are still in school). If you are starting to see a significant gang problem in your library, you should meet with the police and discuss what to do. The cops can use selective enforcement techniques to keep problematic gang members out of your facility.

Mentally Ill Patrons

As one of my security colleagues from Texas puts it, in his usual homespun way, "These are the DLR guys, cuz they Don't Look Right." It's not illegal to be mentally ill. It is a matter for the police if someone in your facility is out of touch with reality, unable to care for his or her own safety, or is a danger to himself or herself or others. You may have a lot of mentally ill patrons who never cause problems, disrupt the business, or even draw attention to themselves. You may have a certain small population of mentally ill people (who may be homeless and substance abusers as well—what you could call "polyproblem patrons") who do hurt your business and do make staff and other patrons feel unsafe.

Problematic mentally ill people are often fearful as well as being aggressive. The world is just too big and too fast for them. As such, be careful not to come too close to them, touch them, or touch their stuff. Use simple questions, instructions, and commands. Ask them to leave for the day. If you or others feel threatened, call the police for help. I discuss how to get more effective help with this difficult population in Chapter 8.

Substance Abusers and Drug Sellers

There are so many ways people can change their physical and mental states with goodies that are distilled, brewed, aged, grown in the ground, or made in a real or filthy lab. George Washington brewed whiskey, as did many of America's founding fathers. Beer and wine go back to the Stone Age, and the ancient Egyptians made mead out of honey. In 2014, archaeologists in China found in the tomb of a Chinese shaman 1.75 pounds of marijuana that he was buried with a short 2,700 years ago. So, clearly, people like to get their buzz on and have done so for quite a while.

It is illegal to be high on drugs and alcohol in public (including inside the library), but some people can control their use, whereas others cannot. Those who cannot are the ones who end up drawing attention to themselves by bothering other people or creating a medical concern that can cause you to ask them to leave, call the police, or call an ambulance. You cannot argue these people into sobriety. Don't try to reason with people who are drunk or high (or both, which makes them especially irrational or physically and verbally unstable). Use space and distance or other proxemic barriers, and don't allow them to come too close to you.

I'm a member of the California Narcotics Officers Association (we have great parties) and we use the acronym SHOCADID to recognize the symptoms of substance abuse:

Stimulants	cocaine, meth, Ritalin, Adderall
Hallucinogens	LSD, Ecstasy, Molly, spice, bath salts, mushrooms
Opiates	heroin, pain pills, Methadone
Cannabis	marijuana, hashish, hash oil
Alcohol	beer, wine, distilled spirits
Depressants	antianxiety, tranquilizers, Valium
Inhalants	paints, solvents, aerosols, gases
Dissociative anesthetics	PCP, Ketamine, Rohypnol, DXM

The drug of choice for violence in this country is alcohol, followed by stimulant drugs, with meth being the biggest concern, all of which can create volatile people who do irrational, paranoid things. As one of my street narcotics cop pals used to ask, "Would you rather live next door to one hundred pot smokers or one meth user? Which one ruins your neighborhood, deprives you of sleep, and lowers your property values?"

Be aware of drug sellers in your library. Creative dope pushers can use the library as a central location. If you see people hanging around and having brief conversations with strangers and then money or goods quickly changing hands, call the police from a safe location. A couple recent stories illustrate this point: In October 2014, Simi Valley, California, police arrested a homeless man for selling heroin inside the public library. He was selling to people in the parking lot and inside the library. Police responding to complaints about drug use and sales in the library arrived and took the man into custody. They found six grams of heroin on him and $1,500 in cash. In June 2014, Sarasota County, Florida, police arrested a homeless couple for making methamphetamine on the grounds of the Jacaranda Public Library in Venice. A twenty-eight-year-old man and a twenty-three-year-old woman were arrested in possession of several bottles of chemicals, stove fuel, batteries, and tubing. They had been living near the library for about a month.

Code of Conduct or Rule Violators

This is a broad category that includes loud cell phone talkers, sloppy eaters, and all-day sleepers. The message is the same: Be firm, fair, consistent, and assertive. The first five times they do something, perhaps they didn't know and/or they're slow learners. Any more times after that and it's a pattern; they are pushing your boundaries to see what they can get away with. No consequences for repeated rule violations and you can guess the rest: More of the same behavior, or worse, when it escalates. If a patron who likes to break the rules knows that he or she can get away with something Monday through Wednesday because either the staff doesn't care or they're too scared to say anything, but not Thursday through Saturday because the staff addresses the problem, then that patron will act out on Monday, Tuesday, and Wednesday. Allowing such a situation to exist is *not* a good example of being firm, fair, consistent, and assertive.

Door-Dashing, Gate-Crashing Thieves

The whole issue of the response by libraries to the theft of their materials in this country disappoints me greatly. Some library people tell me, "Yeah, we have the electronic gates, but we disconnected the alarms a long time ago because patrons kept setting them off." Or they say, "Our security guard used to chase people and make them come back inside with the materials, but then our city attorney [or county counsel] told him to stop." Or I hear, "Yeah, we have discovered that a lot of our valuable materials end up on eBay or Craigslist. What can you do?" In my Perfect Library World, people would be arrested and prosecuted for stealing large amounts of our materials, as happened to the female thief who stole over 2,000 books from several North County libraries in San Diego. She was arrested, prosecuted, and made to pay $7,600 in restitution back to the library branches.

I certainly don't advocate chasing up the street a patron who mistakenly put a book in his or her bag and forgot to check it out with his or her other books when at the circulation desk. But if a teenager comes in and grabs two armloads of DVDs and runs out, you shouldn't just shrug your shoulders and go back to work. Write down the teen's description, try to determine how he or she left (car, bike, skateboard, on foot), and call the police. Convenience store employees are told by their managers and owners to call the police whenever someone grabs a case of beer or a carton of cigarettes and runs for it. The same should be true for the library. Word on the streets gets around. If the small-time hoods who steal from the library know that the cops get called every time, this provides a real deterrence factor. If they know the cops never get called, then they file that away for future reference as well.

I know the cops are always busy and in many cities won't send an officer for the theft of some DVDs and books; they often take those reports over the phone. Still, they had better send a cop if a thief steals a patron's or employee's laptop, cell phone, or tablet.

Homeless

While speaking with me, a colleague who is a hotel security manager at a downtown San Francisco hotel said it accurately: "Most homeless people are used to being told to leave or move along, by employees, supervisors, security officers, or the police. They get the drill. If they can leave with some of their dignity intact, it helps quite a lot."

In Chapter 8, I discuss how to make the most of your partnership opportunities with government or community-based entities that work with and for the homeless. For now, consider a possible solution to a common and ongoing problem, which is when groups of homeless people "take up residence" at your library, coming in at opening time and staying into the evening, often by commandeering the same tables and chairs in the library each day. Here, they hold court, swap stories, and generally make themselves at home. This gathering of street people, along with their bags and bags of things, can create an enclave in your library where most patrons and even some staff are fearful to enter. So, what do you do?

One approach I suggest that has worked is to hold a Summit Meeting of sorts with the one or two of the most vocal ringleaders of this group and get them to agree on following some rules. One library was within sight of a homeless shelter that was open only in the evenings and overnight. A certain chunk of the homeless population would set up shop in the library and wait for nightfall. They ate and slept and, if I had to guess, drank in the library, monopolized the restrooms, and made a lot of patrons flee to other branches. Since we all agreed that their presence hurt the business of being a library, the library director met with several of the group's "spokespeople" and said, in so many words:

> This ends today. You will have to leave the library for extended periods of time and take all your bags, which block our aisles and create a litter problem and a fire hazard, with you. You are all welcome to use the library for legitimate purposes, like everyone else, but you can't just hang out here all day, every day. I've already talked to the police department, and they have promised to send officers in here every day to talk with you about leaving. They will run people for warrants and make arrests for being drunk or high on drugs. If they have to take you to jail, they will impound your stuff. Do we have an agreement about using our library?

The message was sent and received. The daytime campouts ended. This strongly worded message was the result of lengthy and good dialogues between the library's leadership and the police department beforehand.

The Hygienically Challenged

Discussing personal hygiene is a difficult conversation to have with a patron, but it's a crucial one because someone's bad hygiene can hurt the business of the library. Disregard for personal hygiene often stems from depression or other mental illnesses, a medical condition or a side effect of certain medications (or meth use), religious beliefs (rarely), or dementia or other cognitive impairments related to old age. Starting your day with a friendly chat with a patron who has a hygiene problem is hardly what any library staffer or supervisor looks forward to, but it may be necessary.

The business impact reason, or how this issue hurts the business of the library in a negative way, can't be denied. It's a given that this conversation should take place in a private place on the library floor (sit downwind if you can). The staffer or supervisor can start by saying, "This is an uncomfortable yet necessary part of my job. As hard as this is to talk about, I have some concerns that your body odor is making it hard for other people to be around you. I've seen for myself that it's affecting our staff and other patrons in a way that is not good for our business. I'm sure it's embarrassing for you and it's not my intention to make you feel worse. Starting right away, if you want to use the library, you need to come in clean and smelling better." If the patron in this discussion is clearly homeless, perhaps you can provide bus tokens or passes to day-use shelters where the person can have a shower and get cleaned up.

Service Animal versus Comfort Animal Arguers

Writing for the October 20, 2014, issue of *The New Yorker*, in her piece "Pets Allowed," Patricia Marx showed the ongoing semantic battle between people with legitimate, trained, card-carrying service animals and the growing movement in favor of people who now bring their emotional support/comfort animals everywhere they go. Her article is insightful, funny, and a tad disturbing, as she recounted her own travels with animals. Marx brought an alpaca to a drugstore (and almost on board Amtrak for a train trip from Hudson, New York, to Niagara Falls). She took a pig on a plane flight to and from Boston, and to the Four Seasons Hotel there for high tea. She took a tortoise on a leash into the Frick Collection, a museum in Manhattan, and then to a ritzy shoe store, a nail salon, a chocolate shop, and, finally, a funeral home. She took a snake into the NYC Chanel store, two restaurants, and a movie theater. She brought a twenty-six-pound turkey on an NYC tour bus and then to a deli (where I'm guessing there was no discussion of a certain cold cut on the menu).

This whole issue has become a legal hot potato. In my Perfect Library World, patrons with trained service dogs can come inside and homeless guys with ever-snarling pit bulls cannot. Got a guide dog for a blind or disabled patron? Please come this way. Want to bring in a comfort snake, weasel, ferret, guinea pig, rat, cat, bat, or Shetland pony? I'm sorry, but no can do. (Rent the classic Bill Murray–Richard Dreyfuss comedy *What About Bob?* to see Murray, in full anxiety mode, bringing his emotional support fish—named Gil, of course—with him on a bus in a jar of water around his neck.) I say *no* means *no*, but get some sound and hopefully courageous legal advice from your city attorney or county counsel on this ever-evolving matter.

Internet Hogs

I'm a fan of a structured process for Internet use, including a one-hour time limit that cuts the screen; a separate Internet usage card beyond just a library card; a sign-in sheet for using it each time; privacy screens; content-filtering systems; and a rights-and-rules screen the patron must click on before use.

I'm not a fan of government intrusion on Internet use in general, save for stopping criminal activities, terrorism, and child sexual exploitation. But I do believe libraries must have some ground rules in place to create reasonable boundaries for appropriate patron use. Hogs try to monopolize time on the system and thereby prevent other people from using the computers. Having a usage structure in place and a staffer in that area who gives reminders about time limits in a firm tone can help a lot with the patron who seems to forget, each time he or she signs on, what the rules of use are.

Internet Weirdos/Porn Enthusiasts

I'm asked this question all the time in libraries: "What do we do with the guy [and it's always a man] who logs on and brings up all kinds of provocative imagery and then seems to take great delight in seeing if he can offend adults or children who are walking by?" Go back to my previous points about the benefits of time limits, filtering, and privacy screens with Internet hogs; the same approaches can help here.

If such a usage structure is not possible in the current library culture or forthcoming in the next budget cycle, my usual security or behavioral measure is to move the computer screens so that they don't all face outward toward the floor. Many libraries I go to seem to favor putting the Internet-using patron with his or her back to the floor. The user faces a wall, and the rest of the world gets to see what is on the screen. In my Perfect Library World, the majority of Internet users would sit in small cubicles (not designed like peep-show booths, of course), with dividers and privacy screens so that they face out and the screens face the wall. This makes it harder to offend people who are walking by, but library staff can still see what is going on as they pass. I realize that it isn't possible to orient the entire library this way, but I have seen facilities where the majority of the Internet screens are flipped in this fashion.

As to the primary issue of objectionable content (mostly related to pornographic pictures and videos), I have seen library people take strong positions on both sides of addressing the issue with patrons. Some say, "I stop it as soon as I see it. I threaten to kick them off the computers or revoke their Internet use cards if it continues. These guys know absolutely what they're doing and they didn't get to a porn site by accident. I tell them they have to be respectful of the library and the other people here, including staff, or they're gone." At the other end of the spectrum are those who say, "We've been told not to address it. It's their choice and it's a free country. As long as they aren't bothering females or children, we can't do anything about what they display. When we tell them not to do it, they rudely tell us to leave them alone."

I'm a big fan of courage. If you work in a facility where the second response is more the norm, work together with your colleagues to move toward implementing the first solution.

Possible or Actual Pedophiles

With the passage of Megan's Law in 1994, it became possible for anyone with access to a computer to go online to the Megan's Law sex offender website for his or her state. These databases were created with the intention of helping people identify those men (and a few women) who have been convicted of certain sexually related crimes and who, as a condition of their probation or parole (in some cases, they are not allowed to live near or visit places where children are, like schools), agreed to register as a sex offender, often for life. Not registering is a felony in many states, which is why you should call the police anytime you have concerns that an adult stranger is making frequent contact with a child in or near the library.

Normal adult males don't strike up long and intrusive conversations with children they don't know in public places, restrooms, parks, or the library. They don't let children climb on their laps, play video games with them, or invite them to lunch at a nearby McDonald's—all are the so-called grooming behaviors of manipulative pedophiles. If what you see doesn't feel right to you intuitively, then you should discuss your concerns with your boss or colleagues and then with the police. The police will contact the person to verify whether there is a legitimate reason for him to be near a child, and if the person is not currently registered as a sex offender but should be, has an outstanding warrant, or is in violation of his probation or parole requirements, then he will be arrested. This is not about making rash value judgments, designed to accuse people or ruin their lives; it's about using an existing system to keep kids who come to your facility safe from potentially harmful people they may not know are near them.

Domestic Violence Perpetrators or Stalkers

These are different fruits from the same tree. And the sad reality is that domestic violence victims could be library employees or library patrons. The perpetrators can be current or former boyfriends or girlfriends, current or former spouses or domestic partners, or the estranged parents of children. As with most issues around violence, men are statistically the most common perpetrators in domestic violence crimes, but that doesn't mean women can't commit violent acts as well. If you witness a domestic violence situation involving a patron and his or her partner, keep other people out of the way, get to a safe location, and call 911.

I tell all employees in my training programs that if they have a current restraining order against anyone who could come to the library and violate the order, they need to tell their supervisor and the library director so that they can respond with a work safety plan and efforts to best protect the employee, which may include moving him or her to a new location or taking him or her off the floor. Only eight states in the United States, including my home state of California, have laws on the books mandating that an employer cannot fire a person based on learning that he or she is a victim of domestic violence. In other less-enlightened states, a boss can say, "Don't drag your personal life into work," and fire the employee. Now the employee has two problems: No job and a scary partner who might harm him or her. Domestic violence perpetrators are volatile and dangerous, which makes their arrival at the library to confront their former partners reason for an urgent police call.

Laws in all fifty states define stalking as a pattern of menacing behavior that involves one person following, calling, harassing, or intimidating another person over a span of time, behavior that places the harassed person in reasonable, sustained fear for his or her safety. In threat management, we define stalking subjects in two ways. The most volatile situation is when a love relationship has ended and the suspect is trying to get his or her former partner to restart the relationship, and when this fails, the person engages in harassment, threats, vandalism, or actual violence. Less likely to include violence but just as problematic is the situation in which there was no previous intimate relationship but the suspect wants to start one.

An example of the second type is the guy who brings a female library staffer flowers, candy, stuffed animals, or often highly inappropriate gifts, like expensive jewelry or high-dollar gift certificates, as if they are already in a long-term relationship. This can be flattering at first, but then it just turns creepy when Mr. Right Now doesn't take no for an answer. If the victim says she already has a husband or a boyfriend or does not want to date the suspect, he just nods his head and tries harder to "win her over." Frank talks from the library director or a supervisor about leaving the employee alone, now and forever, often fall on the stalker's tone-deaf ears. Even being contacted by the police does not deter him because, most likely, he suffers from an obsessional belief that is often delusional: "This person wants me. She just doesn't know it yet, so I need to double down on the number of e-mails, texts, and phone calls I send her way."

Restraining orders are most useful in situations involving no previous sexual intimacy between the victim and the suspect. They don't work as well with former intimate partners, especially if the suspect has a poor history of following the rules. Whether you have the first type of stalker or the second, these cases will require police involvement.

Patrons Who Engage in Sexual Behaviors

Sad to say, but I can count on the fingers and toes of my hands and feet the number of female library employees who have told me some idiot exposed himself or engaged in sexual behavior in front of them while on the job. This paraphilia behavior is not only crude and illegal; it also foreshadows a concern that police and sex crimes detectives have about the escalation of a suspect's actions. Their boredom after a while with various high-risk public sex acts leads to their thinking about raising the stakes: Today the stacks at the local library, next week standing at a woman's bedroom window while she sleeps, and a month after that a sexual assault. You must report any sex crimes that happen to you or a patron to the police immediately and create a Security Incident Report.

Entitled Parents

"How dare you speak to [accuse, kick out, etc.] my son [daughter] that way" is often the favorite phrase of entitled parents. My best advice when dealing with angry, entitled parents who come back to the library to find out what happened or who confront you if you speak to their child about library rules is to separate them from their kids before you talk with them. If there are two parents and one child, ask politely, "Dad, could you stay with your son over there for a moment while I talk with your wife over here?" or "Mom, could you wait with your daughter for just a minute while I speak with your husband over here?" And if there is only one parent, ask him or her, "Is it okay if your son [or daughter] waits nearby while you and I step over here to talk?"

Separating the parties is a good idea anytime you need to have a crucial conversation. And as you well know, especially if you have kids yourself and feel as (overly) protective about them as I do for mine, it's easy to get angry and emotional about how they are treated (even if they were the instigators of the problems). It's just easier to talk with one parent than it is to have both of them chirping at you. Similarly, it's hard to have an adult conversation if the child hears everything and chimes in, "That's not true! She's a liar! It didn't happen that way!"

Let the parent you're speaking to vent for a bit, validate his or her concerns that the child was not singled out or mistreated, and see if you can come to an understanding. It's possible you or another library staffer made a mistake in handling the situation previously, in which case, own up and apologize. It's also more likely that the parent didn't get all the facts or the whole truth from the child, and you can gently but firmly explain the real deal. Parents won't always believe you or go away happy, but if you manage the conversation by being professional and without losing your cool, they may realize (probably not until the drive home) that you were right and their kid was wrong.

Non-English Speakers

Why do we speak to people who don't speak any English as if they were deaf or stupid? We have a noticeable tendency to shout at them or add "o" to the end of every sentence: "You need to wait over there-o, sir-o. Thank you-o." The useful and ancient Golden Rule says treat people the way you want to be treated. The more useful and modern Platinum Rule says treat people the way *they* want to be treated. There's a significant difference between the two approaches. If I speak only Spanish and you speak only English, the Golden Rule for you would dictate that I should speak to you in English, the way *you* would want someone to speak to you, but for me, Spanish would be the language to use. The Platinum Rule says that you should find me a Spanish speaker; solve my problem my way, not your way.

At the next staff meeting, if you don't already know, ask what languages your colleagues speak besides English (and the sweet language of the Dewey Decimal System). You may be surprised to find a diversity of different tongues that could be useful in a situation (especially in an emergency) where knowing one of those languages would be helpful.

In any situation for which you might need a translator to help a patron better understand what you're saying, don't be shy about asking out loud, in the room or over the PA, "Does anyone here speak Tagalog [or Russian or Vietnamese, etc.]?" You can try to get the person's nearby family members to translate; sometimes they speak both languages fluently. In a medical or police emergency, call 911 and ask the dispatcher if anyone in the call center speaks the language you need.

Unruly Teenagers

The divide-and-conquer rule works here, similar to what I advised earlier when dealing with two parents. Because of their blanket immaturity, constant anxiety about fitting in, and collision between puberty, hormones, and feeling able to sass back at adults who aren't their parents, teenagers, especially in a group, can be trying. Identify the ringleader of the group and ask him or her to meet you over to the side, out of earshot of his or her peers. My favorite phrase, one I use constantly with all types of patrons who are not complying, is this: "You can't keep doing that if you want to stay here. Can you go back and tell your friends, please?"

This phrase works because it gives the person a face-saving way out of the situation. "Fine! We'll just leave then!" is the answer you're looking for. Whether directed at a homeless guy trying to push his shopping cart full of stuff into your library, a mentally ill patron causing a scene, or a group of teenagers making rude comments to people, the phrase "You can't do that if you want to stay here" is a showstopper. You're not ordering them to stop, but it's not up for debate either. If they say, "Yeah? What are you going to do if we don't?," then you have some choices: Asking security to escort them out, if you have a guard; pulling their names and contact information and calling their parents to discuss their behavior at a later date; or if the situation becomes hostile enough, leaving and calling the police to have them escorted out for disturbing the peace or trespassing. You can't win a group argument with them, so disengage, get some help, and come back with a new plan.

Small Children

There is a disparity sometimes between the different patience levels of patrons when it comes to tolerating what most of us would classify as normal kid behavior. Some patrons smile and think nothing of a noisy or rambunctious child in the library. Others are offended if one kid makes a single peep. The culture of your library dictates your response to children, as does the context of their activities. If a patron complains about kids laughing and joining in during a reading program, I'd politely tell the person to go back home and look for that box where he or she must've accidentally packed away his or her humanity. Conversely, kids who can't control themselves or won't be controlled by their erstwhile parents might need one or more reminders about appropriate behavior.

I once heard a story about a kid running amok in a library as the mother stood there, next to a library staffer, doing nothing. The staffer said, "Mom, would you like me to talk to your son about good library behavior or do you want to?" This is an absolutely awesome question because it both puts the mom on notice that it's time to be a parent and, if she doesn't want to, allows the employee to correct the kid without embarrassing the mother.

Abandoned Children

The world is always changing when it comes to kids and parents and maturity and responsibility. My parents dropped me off at places when I was a kid, and I would walk long distances back home. Most times they didn't know where my friends and I were. Then there was the Overprotective Period during which parents wouldn't let their kids play in their own front yards or take a bus alone or go to the mall without an armed escort from the Green Berets. Now society has evolved to the point at which every kid on the planet above age eight has a cell phone and knows how to use Google Maps better than most adults.

There is a big difference between a young child who has a cell phone, a bike, or a bus pass and a good head on his or her shoulders being in your library versus a kid who gets dropped off by his or her erstwhile parent and who cannot take care of himself or herself and shouldn't be left alone. The first one acts with confidence; the second one wanders around your facility all day and into the night basically unsupervised (though you hope nothing bad happens to him or her, you aren't being paid to watch one child). Some of these so-called parents give their kids a can of soda and a candy bar and say, "Hang out in the library for the day, little Johnnie. I'll see you in fifteen hours. If they kick you out of the library, go to the park."

Related to the issue of putting a child at risk is the problem of the parent who uses the library for free day care and then shows up late to pick up the kid, several minutes or even hours after closing time. I have seen well-meaning library employees sit for hours with a child they didn't know on the front steps of the library, waiting for a parent to show up. This is admirable but wrong. If it's near closing time and the child is too young to know the contact numbers for a parent or other responsible family member, is standing alone outside your library, and has no one to come for him or her, or someone comes but is two hours late, consider calling the police and reporting an abandoned child. If you don't, you will create in this alleged parent's mind the sense that it's okay to use the library staff for free child care. Such behavior demands consequences. Let the parent explain to a cop and a social worker where he or she was while this too-young child sat cold, hungry, and alone in a public building all day, day after day.

Elderly, Disabled, or Dependent Adults

Perhaps my biggest concern for these patrons is not their potential for behavioral issues, which tend to be more about needing more help than other patrons and not being able to get it, but rather the chances that they could be victimized by opportunistic thieves, scam artists, and those who target this population for financial or physical abuse. There are horrible so-called caregivers out there who prey upon these people, and you may see interactions between them at your library. If you suspect elder or dependent adult abuse, get as much information as you can about all parties and make a report to your county's Adult Protective Services (APS) agency.

Some elderly patrons may not be as comfortable with the speed and pace of technology in your branch, so they sometimes require extra time and attention from you to be able to get what they need. Patience is useful and necessary when dealing with all three of these patron types.

Patrons Who Want Tax or Legal Advice

The tax advice seeker appears in your library on January 2, looking for tax forms. Even if you happen to have these forms in your facility, by the next week, they're back for more forms and now they have questions. These questions aren't of the "Where are the 1040EZ forms?" type. No, they are more like this: "Can I deduct my dog's vet bills since he's technically an employee of my limited liability corporation?" And when such questions are met with the best answer a library staffer or supervisor can give—"Sorry, but we don't give tax advice"—now begin the howls of outrage as to why not. There is no other answer in these situations, so put on that broken record and don't overexplain.

Your law library colleagues suffer the same fate, but only times a thousand and only all year long. Some of the most persistent "answer my tax and legal question" patrons suffer from what my psychology colleagues call "perseveration," which means they are obsessed with the same theme and they can't not talk about it. Law library employees, who may also be real lawyers, are forbidden by their bar associations from giving legal advice. There are signs posted everywhere in the law library that echo this true and immutable fact, and yet, day after day, the same questions come in about pro per lawsuits, quickie divorces, and filing for bankruptcy over the phone. Repeat the same answer as with the tax seeker, until it sinks in, which for some patrons may be as soon as never.

Employees with "Issues"

Okay, so employees aren't patrons—consider this a bonus category—but they are part of the library's community and can therefore affect the library's business. You may work with coworkers who live what could be accurately defined as "highly complicated lives." Three little letters can help them: EAP. I am a big believer in the power and benefit of Employee Assistance Programs to help employees deal with their personal and professional stressors.

When I discuss the value of EAP counseling with employees, some are unaware of the services that an EAP provides, some don't understand that participation in the program is completely confidential, and some don't realize that they can work with a therapist over the phone, face-to-face in the therapist's office, or even at the library. I have brought in EAP counselors to work with library employees who are domestic violence victims, using their lunch hours as the time to have confidential meetings in an unused office. Why? Because they are afraid their batterers would find out they were seeking help, I brought the therapists to them to preserve the confidentiality of the process.

And while some employees may not understand how EAP services work, it pains me to hear that other employees are not even aware that their city or county offers an EAP as part of their employee benefits. The list of subjects covered by EAP counselors is long and includes the plethora of personal and work stressors that can affect an employee on and off the job.

This includes help with financial or legal problems, marital issues, blended families, stepchildren, substance abuse issues, gambling addictions, cancer diagnoses, sick parents, or depression. I have seen these services save employees' lives and careers, so I'm a believer in the resources. If you're a supervisor, or you want to be one someday, EAP referrals are a good tool for your toolkit. We can't force employees to go, but we can remind them of the value of reaching out for help before it's too late.

CHAPTER 5

Understanding Threats and Getting Help

Time for a counterintuitive question: Would you rather deal with a patron who acts like a maniac in your library, yelling at other patrons and threatening staff, or with a patron who makes an ominous statement, half under his or breath—"This isn't over"—and leaves? I'll take the first one, every time. Why? Because the first one is a Howler and the second one might be a Hunter.

Identifying Hunters and Howlers

Dr. Fred Calhoun, a former historian for the US Marshals Service and retired deputy director at the Transportation Security Administration, and Steve Weston, former commander in charge of the California Highway Patrol's Dignitary Protection Detail, have done significant research, extensive training, and lots of writing to support their groundbreaking model of Hunters versus Howlers, which talks about two uniquely different sets of preattack behaviors: Some people *howl* (make overt threats, draw attention to themselves, frighten others intentionally) but don't hunt, and some people *hunt* (develop a hidden plan, acquire the weapons to harm others, work in stealth, and attack with little or no warning) but don't howl. In other words, we have more to be concerned about from people who *don't* make threats than from those who do.

As the US Secret Service has echoed in its 1998 groundbreaking research as part of the Exceptional Case Study Project, many people *make* threats, some people *pose* threats. The people who make threats are less likely to act on them than are those who pose threats. While the Secret

Service *talks* to Howlers, who even call its National Threat Assessment Center to say they want to kill the President, it *looks* for Hunters. While the Secret Service actively manages both types of people, it is the Hunters who keep agents up at night, worried that these perpetrators will move, as described in the research, "along a path from ideas to actions."

Howlers howl to make people fearful, appear provocative, draw attention to themselves or their causes, feel important and superior, and disrupt business. Hunters stalk their targets, make detailed plans, acquire and practice with weapons, and try to hurt or kill people. Howlers make bomb threats to schools, malls, churches, businesses, and government offices. Hunters create explosive devices, test them, and detonate them against a chosen target, all without warning.

In their book *Threat Assessment and Management Strategies: Identifying the Howlers and Hunters* (CRC Press, 2009), Calhoun and Weston redefine a threat management concept that Dr. Calhoun has espoused for many years: Howlers howl and Hunters hunt. That is, although we have much to do when managing the behavior of a Howler, who is visible, emotional, outwardly aggressive, bothersome, and into attention-getting and fear-creating behaviors, we are less likely to see the Howler's behavior erupt into workplace violence. It is the Hunters who move on to what they call "the path to intended violence" by engaging in stealth behaviors, designed not to call attention to themselves but to make it more likely that they can attack without warning and without being stopped. The authors refer to this path by its parts: Grievance (the reason or motive the Hunter needs to strike); ideations (which make the use of violence justifiable); research and planning (how the Hunter will act); preparation (acquiring weapons or taking similar actions); breach (where the Hunter defeats the security around the facility or target); and, finally, the attack itself.

And while Hunters typically move toward violent acts and Howlers are usually content to create fear, anxiety, and apprehension in their targets or the organizations where they may have worked or visited, once Howlers change their minds and step on the path to intended violence, they cease to be Howlers. This does not mean, Calhoun and Weston contend, that the differences between Howlers and Hunters can be easily prescribed solely by a list of characteristics; these descriptors are not purely concrete, only a well-documented and heavily researched model for understanding pre-attack behaviors (hunting) versus fear-creating acts (howling).

Why don't Hunters howl? They don't want to be stopped or arrested; they want their chance to strike. Why don't Howlers hunt? Except for what's often called the "domestic violence exception," or what researcher Debra Jenkins calls the "intimacy effect," they are not willing to move along the path from *thinking* about violence to *using* violence. But anytime there is previous sexual intimacy between a victim and a suspect, the victim is at significant risk for violence. Every woman on the planet knows it is dangerous for her to hear from a former love partner, "If I can't have you, no one else will."

When I'm involved in a threat assessment case involving a patron who is bothering a female library staffer, my first question is, "How do you know this guy?" I'm less concerned for her physical safety if she says, "I've never seen him before he started showing up here, bringing me little gifts and always asking me out. Whenever I say no, he gets furious and leaves." I'm significantly more concerned for her physical safety if she says, "He's my ex-husband or my ex-boyfriend and he just won't leave me alone. He has hit me before and he says he will hurt me if I don't get back together with him."

In the first example, the person bothering the employee is a growing nuisance that will require the use of a number of tools to get him to leave her alone, including giving him one—and only one—warning to stop his behavior. The next step is to discuss the value of a restraining order if his approaches continue to make the employee afraid to come and go at work. In the second example, the right thing to do is to call the police immediately to make them aware of past and current threatening behaviors. Most cops have seen these cases many times before and they will recognize the potential for volatility here. Another precaution to take in these cases is to move the staffer to a back office position or to another branch while the police attempt to contact the suspect and assess his level of dangerousness.

Assessing and Managing the Threat

Perhaps it's time for a bit of a breather and a reality check about this concept of Hunters versus Howlers. First, the good news: Most people who make threats at libraries are Howlers. They want (negative) attention but have no intention of acting out because they still fear the consequences (getting arrested, losing their freedom, being civilly barred from a place they want to go). The bad news: Hunters act out without making threats and they can be quite dangerous. But here's some better news: Hunters leak. While they don't threaten the target directly, they do tell other people. This third-party leakage is what helps police catch them and stop them from acting out.

We can see countless examples of this leakage when looking at the aftermath of workplace or school violence incidents. Prior to engaging in school violence, the students who want to shoot their teachers do not threaten the teachers directly, as this would be Howler behavior. When around the teachers, the students may even be quiet and respectful. But when around their peers, the students will make threats to kill teachers, and the opportunity to stop them occurs when their friends tell others inside or outside the school, including other kids, teachers, school security, or counselors they trust or their parents or friends' parents. Once the cat is out of the bag, the process to identify and talk to those students moves quite quickly, as we all have seen when similarly foiled plots make the news.

In a potential workplace violence situation, the actions of the Howler are to make verbal threats about shooting up the place, whereas the actions of the Hunter are to make quiet remarks about doing so to others around him or her, even in ways that might not be identified until the aftermath of a tragedy. Again, this leakage is what leads to interventions through police responses, security measures, or mental health evaluations.

Why do Hunters leak? First, not all of them do. For my workplace violence book *Ticking Bombs* (Irwin, 1994), I interviewed Robert Mack in a California prison. He shot two people during a termination hearing in 1992 at General Dynamics in San Diego and never told a soul his plan—not his girlfriend, not his coworkers, no one in his family, nobody. But perhaps these are some of the reasons Hunters leak: They just can't help themselves because they feel that they have to tell someone; they want the people they tell to either talk them out of it, thereby giving them a face-saving reason not to harm someone, or perhaps encourage them to do it—"Yeah, shoot that teacher. I hate him too."

Here's the bottom line when it comes to managing threats: There are no guarantees that all Howlers merely howl and all Hunters hunt or always leak. Threat assessment and management are driven by the behaviors of the potential perpetrators, and we may never know why they acted out or didn't act out. Since it's hard to prove a negative, we won't always know what we did or said or didn't do or didn't say that stopped them. We do know that Howlers can be identified, managed, controlled, and stopped far easier than Hunters.

Most of the people who cause a scene at the library are Howlers. Respond to them with good customer (high-risk) service skills, security policies, and help from your safety and security stakeholders.

Calling the Police

There are two important reasons to call the police for assistance with problematic patron situations: To get the cops to help you enforce consequences for the situations, and for them to be able to do what they do best, which is to preserve the peace and lower the emotional temperature. We'd like to think that the police drive around or walk around all day and night fighting crime, but more realistically, they keep the social fabric from tearing by being visible, approachable, and responsive in situations where their presence solves the presenting crime or violence problems or simply calms things down. We call the police for high-risk patron situations to send an ongoing and unmistakably clear message to those people that it's not all right to fight, threaten, or stalk people, it's not okay to be drunk or high and disrupt the business, and it's wrong to steal or damage the library's materials or property or the personal property of others. And we call them to show up and take control of situations where their presence sends a message to all patrons who are acting out: "The cops just got here. Either I keep my mouth shut and stop doing what I'm doing or they will haul me off to jail." Don't underestimate the value of this tool for you to keep your library safe.

In my Perfect Library World, we would use code words to tell one another to go to a safe place and call the police. If you are in a situation where your intuition suggests that you should call the police, then you should be prepared to do so. But avoid the temptation to tell the problem patron that you will call the cops. "If you say one more thing or you do that again, then I'm calling the police!" One reason you might want to say this is in the hope that the person who is causing the problem will leave, which makes sense from a safety and security perspective; it would be better if the person left on his or her own. The problem with making the "I'm calling the cops" announcement is that it may trigger a violent reaction from the person on the receiving end of that news.

Consider what might be going on inside a patron's boozy, fuzzy head: "The cops? Uh-oh. I'm high on drugs [or hooch] right now. I've got some drugs on me. I've got a warrant. I'm already on probation or parole. Maybe they know about that thing I did last week." Given those thoughts, the person may decide to hit you, run off, or hit you and then run off: "If I'm going to go to jail anyway, I might as well smack you a good one for calling the cops." And if the person is significantly mentally ill, he or she might believe that the cops will hurt or kill him or her when they arrive and take out their handcuffs.

Thus, my usual advice is to use code words to send another coworker to a safe place, out of earshot of the patron, and then get the police on the line. I typically suggest the code words "Mr. Blue or Dr. Blue," since cops often wear blue uniforms. In my state, most sheriff's deputies wear tan shirts and green pants, so we use "Mr. Green or Dr. Green" for libraries in a sheriff's territory. The code words you choose don't have to be based on uniform colors ("Go page Dr. Khaki" sounds odd), so pick a phrase everyone can agree on and remember, even in the stress of the moment (e.g., "Bring me the purple file folder, please"), that means "Go to a safe place and call the police."

If you're by yourself in the library, you may have to completely disengage from the problem patron and go to a safe place behind a locked door to call the police. Another reason for using code words to alert another staff member to go call the police is that it has a multiplier effect: You continue to deal with the patron, your colleague goes and calls the police, and the next sound the patron hears is the cops jingling up the walkway, radios blaring and sunglasses coming off.

In some situations, your intuition might tell you that it's simply safer to call for police help after the problem patron has left. I don't disagree. Your safety is the primary issue, and if you think it's better to wait to call, then you should wait to call. The only problem with this approach is that the police may arrive five to fifty-five minutes later, depending on where they are and where they're coming from, and they will always ask you the same question: "Which way did he go?" If you point in an outside direction and say, "He went thataway" (just like in old Western movies when the townspeople are talking to the posse), the usual police response will be, "Call us if he comes back." This may or may not solve the presenting problem, which is why I like to train all staff to use code words to summon the police immediately after you decide they're needed.

Since we were little kids, we've been taught to use 911 to get emergency help. And that's always true, except when it isn't. With some phone systems, you must dial 9 first to get an outside line and then 911. In emergencies, some people who forget to dial 9 first get a busy signal or extension 11, neither of which is what they want. Under stress, we go back to how we have been trained. If you've not preprogrammed yourself to dial 9 first, you may forget under the stress of the situation. Write 9-911 on your telephone box or post little signs near your phone to remind you and everyone else.

Consider also the ubiquitous cell phone. Most people have their electronic umbilical cord within five feet of them, twenty-four hours a day. (If you don't sleep next to your cell phone, you're in the minority in this world.) Dialing 911 on a cell phone in most parts of my state will connect you with the California Highway Patrol, which may not be your first choice for a police emergency. There could be a substantial delay while the state police in your area connect you to the local police or sheriff's dispatchers. The problem with this issue of who answers your cell phone emergency call is that it's not uniform around the country. Depending on the pace of technology in your area, your cell call could get answered by your local police or sheriff's department, who may know, because of GPS (Global Positioning System) mapping, where you are within 150 feet. Other systems rely on the state police or a combination of county fire and law enforcement agencies in a primary dispatch center. It's important to know who answers cell call emergencies because it may change whether you call from your cell phone or a landline.

The benefit of using a library landline is that it usually automatically shows the dispatcher the address where the call originated. I say "usually" because if you work in a city hall–type complex and the main phone lines are not trunked into your library, then the dispatcher may see only a generic number for all city hall phones and not for your specific building. As such, it's critical to train everyone in the library to tell the dispatcher your exact address, floor, and location on that floor. Under stress, employees will shout, "I'm at the library!" and if there are seven in town, the follow-up question is always, "Which one?" Give the correct and full information straight away and make it easier on yourself, the dispatcher, and the responding cops (who get updated messages about your situation from the dispatchers on their patrol car mobile data terminals as they head your way). Tell the dispatcher who you are, where you are, and who is causing the problem. When talking to a dispatcher, it's important to describe behaviors and not use labels. "There's a crazy guy in our lobby!" or "There's a nut in our parking lot!" may be technically true, but these don't describe the problems.

Once you've called the police about a patron, if you can, wait from a place of safety (with other patrons and staff) for them to arrive. In certain situations where the patron is out of control and threatening people with or without a weapon, you may need to take people (staff and patrons) to a safe place behind a locked door. Be a professional witness, and if the patron has left, give the police an accurate description—race and gender; approximate age, height, and weight; as much detail about his or her clothing, tattoos, or other identifying characteristics as you can remember; weapons or other belongings; the make, model, color, and license plate of a car, if used; and the last direction of travel.

On a procedural note, the police can arrest someone for a misdemeanor only if it's committed in their presence. If the patron is drunk or high on drugs or has an outstanding warrant when they get there, they will handle it because the evidence is in front of them. But if you call the cops because a drunk patron has broken a table worth $200, you will have to sign the citizen's arrest form for misdemeanor vandalism. If the patron does $2,000 worth of damage to your library, the cops can arrest him or her for felony vandalism themselves. Some employees are afraid, don't want to get involved, and won't sign a citizen's arrest form, fearing retaliation from the suspect if they do. This is a mistake. If you don't sign the arrest form, the cops may not be able to do very much if the misdemeanor crime was not committed in front of them. Do you want them to take the patron away for what he or she did or just give him or her a stern lecture not to return again? You know that if there are no consequences for the behavior, it will continue or escalate. Do the right thing and sign the form.

The Great Debate: Are Security Guards Needed in the Library?

As a good consultant, whenever I don't know the answer to a question, which happens more than I will admit, I always say, "It depends." As for the question of the need for uniformed security guards or, as I have seen in some library locations, on-duty police officers or sheriff's deputies, working overtime, the answer is a well-qualified "It depends."

In my Perfect Library World, where money is not a factor and I am given a choice between having one or more security guards on the property, I would say yes most every time. But even this scenario has its limitations.

The quality of the chosen security company and the training, vigilance, and excellent customer service skills required for its guards are no small matter. As celebrity security expert Gavin de Becker has so aptly put it, "When it comes to certain security officers, sometimes we are protected *by* people we should be protected *from*." He says this with no malice in his heart but only from the proof that comes from the reality that is the private security world.

The disconnect between the security guard supplier and the security guard customer is often a wide one. The client wants a former US Navy SEAL, with weapons skills, combat first-aid training, and a steely eye. The security company says it can certainly supply said officer, which ends up meaning you may get a guy, in some states, who was working at a gas station last week. The big culprit here is pay. It's not that the security salespeople lie because they want to; they lie because they have to. Most security companies "keystone" the pay for their guards, meaning they charge the client $20 per security officer hour and pay the guard $10 per hour. Some guard companies provide much better pay, usually when they are staffed by off-duty police who work on the side; the client pays $70 to $100 per security officer hour and the cops get $35 to $50 per hour. The higher wage is warranted because of their training and because they can work armed.

Back in the real world at the library, we see much less tactical knowledge and professionalism if the guard of choice is not currently a cop picking up some extra cash. And maybe those skills aren't necessary if the library director and the guard company can collaborate on a realistic, balanced set of posted orders for the guards on duty to follow and pass down to the next shift. As the client, you have the right to ask whether (and to expect) the security company you choose is licensed in your state (request a copy of the license), insured (request from the company's insurance broker valid copies of its insurance certificate), and compliant with any state-mandated training required for the licensure of its guards. At a minimum, guards should have powers-of-arrest training as well as CPR (cardiopulmonary resuscitation), AED (automated external defibrillator), and first-aid training. You also have the right to ask the guard company to switch out officers who don't follow your standards or the posted orders.

You want guards with good service skills, not just a bouncer's muscles. You want guards who are physically fit enough to walk regularly through the inside and around the outside of your facility, not just sit at a desk and watch people or cameras. And you want guards who will take action when necessary, not just fall back on the usual mantra in the security world, which is "We observe and report." They should be willing and able to ask aggressive homeless people to leave, quiet noisy teenagers, intervene safely and without violence if they see patrons stealing library material, check both restrooms on a regular basis, escort patrons or employees to their cars after hours, and help create an environment where patrons and employees feel safe and problematic people are less likely to act out.

And in the event of a crime, security guards should be trained and ready to make a citizen's arrest and detain the person until the arrival of the police. This last sentence grays the hair of city attorneys and county counsels when I bring it up. Consider these questions: A patron punches an employee in front of the security officer. Should the security officer head straight to a phone at the circulation desk to call the police, describing what he or she saw, as the aggressor walks out of the building? Or should the security officer detain this person physically, tell someone else to call the police, and hold the assaulter until the police arrive?

People have strong feelings about this issue, on both sides. Library or city or county senior management worry about liability for false arrests, but the law says that every person has the right to make a citizen's arrest for a misdemeanor committed in his or her presence. The police can't arrest someone for a misdemeanor they did not see, only for a felony. But what is the message to the library staff, and especially to the employee who was punched, if the library has a security guard but the officer does nothing? This is the reason guards should be trained in the powers of arrest before they get their security guard card—so they know how to do their jobs!

Security officers have two important tasks: Watching to make sure that staff and patrons are safe but also *intervening* to make sure they are safe. This doesn't mean they get in fights or grab people indiscriminately, but that they are trained, licensed, and supported by their company and by the library to protect people until the police get there.

Let's change the scenario slightly. Let's say you own a jewelry store that has been robbed several times. You hire an armed, uniformed security officer to stand guard so your employees, your customers, and your merchandise are protected from robbers. The guard is trained and certified to use a firearm as a condition of his or her work there, qualifying at a pistol range before receiving his or her license to carry an exposed firearm. A robber comes into your store with a gun. Should your armed guard engage with the robber, using deadly force if there is no other way, or go to the phone and call the police? I hope we all agree that if he or she is armed and facing an armed assailant, the guard should try to stop the robber, using deadly force if necessary.

Many security officers are given the wrong mission: Protect us but don't actually do anything to protect us. If you hire guards for your library, you need to give them very specific orders, place limitations, offer guidance, and provide training as to what to do and not do. Stopping people from harming staff or patrons through the use of physical force, if no other verbal method has worked, or moving people away prior to an attack should be options for them. If not, ask yourself this hard question: "Are we employing security officers to placate staff and patrons into thinking we're a safe facility or will they really help us when we need them to protect us?" What message do you want your staff and patrons to hear?

Perhaps you have the luxury in your budget for one or more security guards in your library. If you don't, you should train all staff members to call the police to get them to preserve the peace, both for crimes that are about to happen and for those which have already happened. Although your security officers may not work directly for your city or county, you should expect them to act like your employees and to treat all patrons the same—firmly, fairly, consistently, and assertively.

Personal Self-Defense

I'm often asked these questions in my library workshops: "Is it ever a good idea to put your hands on any patron?" "Should we ever break up a fight between two patrons?" "Should we ever physically escort anyone out of our building?" The answers to these are simple: "No." "No." And "Hell no." But let's qualify those answers a bit.

You have the right to protect yourself from a physical attack. But if you have been following the precepts in this book, you should already know that this is your last and final option, to be used only if you cannot talk, move, or escape your way out of a confrontation with a patron. The only time I would ever advise you to put your hands on a patron is if he or she physically assaults you, in which case you have the right to defend yourself. This doesn't mean that you have to wait to be struck, grabbed, pushed, or pulled. If you see hands coming toward your head or any part of your body, block them and get out of the way quickly.

The question of breaking up a fight is contextual. Would you seriously ever consider breaking up a fight between two nineteen-year-old men fighting over a girl, access to an Internet computer, a bad drug deal, or a series of hard looks cast across the library floor, when both have twenty-inch biceps and tiny brains? Of course not. I was a cop and I didn't jump into those kinds of altercations. Your best response in such situations is to get to a safe place and call the police. Be a professional witness and watch the proceedings from safety, along with as many patrons and colleagues as you can herd out of the way. You may have some success with yelling, "Stop fighting! Stop fighting! Stop fighting! You have to leave! You have to leave! You have to leave!" in an effort to distract and redirect the two combatants, but it's not guaranteed to work.

Now, back to the context of the situation, if you're a children's librarian and two eight-year-olds are pulling each other's hair, you may decide to physically separate them. But even in this scenario, there are many ways that putting your hands on either or both children can go awry. For example, Albrecht's Law of Unintended Consequences says that you will be punished for doing the right thing when the parents of the two kids try to sue you for "assaulting" their blessed angels. Using your words rather than physical actions (as we are all taught on the playground), separate the children into different parts of the library or the room and call for their parents— is probably a more realistic and less litigious solution. I often tell library staffers, especially ones who work extensively with young children and teens, that they know what works best, based on their experience, intuition, knowledge of the kids, their age, and cultural factors. Just make sure you document your efforts in a Security Incident Report so that you won't be second-guessed by your boss or a parent later.

And as to the question of ever having staff use physical escorts with any patrons, I see nothing but trouble in this approach. (You already know my feelings on having your security officers handle these situations, not staffers.) All a patron has to say is that you injured his or her preexisting shoulder joint problem and you and/or the library will end up paying this person a little or a lot of money to go away. The better alternative is to use noncontact escorts or a "verbal walk and talk," as in, "It's time to leave."

As the police well know, when they arrive on the scene of a confrontation between people and they separate the parties, most people are either verbally resistant (all mouth and loud tones) or physically resistant (not wanting to leave, cooperate, or submit to an arrest). And those people who are physically resistant can be passively resistant (sitting on the ground and refusing to move) or actively resistant (fighting with the cops). When confronted with this type of situation, you need to make these same assessments, and do it quickly.

If the time for talking has passed, if it's too late to discreetly step away, or if your path is blocked by a person who is coming closer and threatening to hit you, then you have the right to defend yourself. In my workshops, I show a slide of two Secret Service agents protecting one of our former presidents at a bookstore signing event. As they stand on either side of him, both agents have their hands in front of them, about midchest, with their fingertips touching and pointing downward and with thumbs pointing upward to create a diamond. They stand with their feet apart, in a slightly bladed stance, one foot just in front of the other. They look balanced and vigilant, just as you would expect. I refer to their posture as "Secret Service Hands"; it's a good model for you to follow when standing face-to-face with hostile or potentially violent people. With your hands in this pose, you look like you're paying attention, you appear to have authority, and you can quickly protect yourself by pushing the combative person away or by quickly moving your hands upward to protect your head and face. (Note how many times you see this same diamond-shaped hand position on talk shows, indicating the person feels confident and really wants to demonstrate his or her expertise.)

The other value to Secret Service Hands is that the posture can serve as a signal to your colleagues that you need immediate help with someone who is making you feel uncomfortable about your safety. When you use this hand position, your colleagues should drop what they are doing and come over to support you by changing the ratios of confrontation. The posture should also signal them to come over to see if they will need to call the police for you from a safe location.

CHAPTER 6

Workplace Violence
Awareness, Prevention, and Response

C ases of workplace shootings inside libraries are rare (but catastrophic), although there have been a few, most recently involving community college, college, or university libraries. Since libraries are public places, are open long hours, and offer lots of ways for people to engage with one another, both positively and negatively, occasional conflict, either directed at staff or between patrons, comes as no surprise to any of us. And since I know of no libraries that screen their patrons for weapons at the front door, we also face the unfixable issue of people bringing legal or illegal guns or knives into our facilities without our knowledge. (I have had conversations with angry library patrons who kept one hand inside their backpacks or pockets while we talked—not a good thing.) Because we can't choose our customers—we get who we get when they come through the door—we have to pay attention to our safety and use our security policies and vigilance to keep everyone safe.

In my threat assessment world, I'm frequently asked to "predict violence." I have to remind the folks around me that this is not possible, by me or any other expert, and the best and most we can do is "assess dangerousness." The good news is that you've been doing this your entire life and are already good at it. As an intuitive creature, you already can read the signs of growing anger in patrons; the key is to not rationalize what you see or worry about being too polite and to get out of harm's way without saying please.

What Is Workplace Violence?

As defined by the media, workplace violence is often connected to the disgruntled ex-employee with a gun who comes back to the business after being terminated. The US Post Office has suffered through its own difficult history with this issue. But the scope of the problem is much broader than just ex-employees; it includes strangers with no connection to the facility; current employees who are injured or killed by their domestic violence partners; students or former students who return to their K–12 schools, colleges, or universities; angry customers or vendors; and even patients at a hospital. (Statistically, hospital emergency departments are some of the most dangerous workplaces in America.)

For library purposes, workplace violence can be better defined as any incident that could do one or more of the following:

- Involve threats of harm or actual violence, including verbal, written, or electronic threats
- Increase in intensity and threaten the safety of an employee, patron, visitor, or vendor
- Create fear for an employee regarding coming to work or staying at work because of his or her concerns about patron threats or violence
- Cause damage, vandalism, or sabotage to the library facility or to an employee's or patron's personal property
- Start at home and cross over to work, as with domestic violence involving an employee's or a patron's current or former partner

The businesses at the highest risk for violence are those which handle cash, operate at night, and are located in high-crime areas. The highest-risk jobs for being killed while at work are police officers, retail store clerks, security officers, and cab drivers. Thankfully, neither libraries nor library employees appear on either list.

Perpetrators of Workplace Violence per OSHA

The federal government keeps track of injuries or murders related to workplace violence through the Department of Labor and its subsidiary, the

Occupational Safety and Health Administration (OSHA; www.osha.gov/SLTC/workplaceviolence). Based on the data, OSHA has created four categories of potential workplace violence perpetrators:

Type 1: Criminals, robbers, or strangers (with no connection to the organization)

Type 2: Taxpayers, customers, patrons, patients, passengers, or vendors (people who receive services from the organization)

Type 3: Current or former employees

Type 4: Current or former spouses/partners of employees

This list of four is actually in the proper order: Type 1 perpetrators account for the most incidents (the majority of cases are robberies), down to Type 4 perpetrators who account for the least. (This fact can be deceiving, however; the leading causes of death for men while at work are accidents and heart attacks, and the leading cause of death for women while on the job is, and has been for many years, murder, either during robberies or related to domestic violence.)

Type 1 incidents are the most prevalent because there are a lot of robberies in this country, some of which end in homicide. Type 2 situations include mass school shootings but also a lot of verbal threats made by customers (and these are just the ones that are reported; consider the millions of verbal threats that aren't ever told to a person or government agency that can record them). Type 3 involves a small number of actual cases but often with horrific, mass murder results. Type 4 scenarios usually involve only two victims (murder-suicide is a common and sad ending to these incidents), so the numbers are small even if the impact is enormous.

Suspicious Activities

Since most workplace violence cases tend to be based on robberies, and many of those start with precrime surveillance, much time is spent during security training reminding retail store clerks to keep their eyes open for precrime casers and for people who are doing things they aren't supposed to do, in places where they're not supposed to be. The same is true in and around your library, where bad people getting ready to do bad things exhibit certain behaviors you need to watch for, discuss with your colleagues and boss, and consider reporting to the police.

As the Department of Homeland Security reminds us, since every citizen is in charge of safety and security in this country, "If You See Something, Say Something!" Look for people in or around the perimeter of your library and parking lots who are doing any of these potentially suspicious behaviors:

- Loitering in unauthorized, restricted, or employee-only areas
- Acting like they are lost
- Refusing to leave when they are asked
- Expressing too much interest in employees
- Scaring others through threatening or irrational behavior
- Leaving quickly after abandoning cars or packages
- Taking photos, videos, or measurements
- Showing too much interest in our activities
- Acting like "vendors" but hanging out in the wrong places or not wearing IDs or uniforms or driving marked vehicles
- Leaving cars in odd locations or driving or leaving overloaded cars

Not everything is a crime or even related to the beginning of a crime; some things you see make complete sense in the context of the situation. When I do site security surveys of library facilities—the same process I'll teach you to do in the next chapter—I bring along library or facilities employees to answer questions about some things I see related to the previous list. They know the building much better than I do, so it helps to have them there to explain things that are being done by people who are strangers to me or to agree with me that a situation is either normal or unusual.

Dr. George Thompson's Verbal Judo: The LEAPS Model

In an update of the late Dr. George Thompson's original 1993 best-selling book, *Verbal Judo: The Gentle Art of Persuasion* (Morrow, 2013), coauthor Jerry Jenkins reminds us of the themes that made this book so useful: Listen carefully to people, especially when they are upset; have empathy, even though you don't always agree with their perspectives; help the other person save face by offering him or her one or more solutions; and be creative in your responses that will meet those goals.

Thompson taught his Verbal Judo seminar to thousands of police officers around the world, first, and then to thousands of people with customer- or public-contact jobs. His work still continues today, even after his passing, through his company, the Verbal Judo Institute (www.verbaljudo.com).

I'm reminded of a story he told in his class when I took it. A giant guy was involved in a bar fight in an Alabama town. Four troopers from the Alabama State Police responded to the bar, saw the size of the guy they needed to arrest, and quickly decided that four of them were not nearly enough. They made a plan to each dive for an arm or a leg on the human beast and hope for the best. As the big man squared off with them to begin the rumble, the senior trooper in the group stopped just before they launched and said to the man, "You're a big guy, and you can probably whip each of us. But you know and we know that, in the end, we'll just keep bringing more guys until you're in handcuffs. I know you don't want to spend time away from your family by going to jail for longer than is required tonight. If we get you in there without a trip to the hospital for any of us, you'll get out before the morning. What do you need from me so that you can go along with the program and you won't get hurt and we won't get hurt?" The bar fighter said, "I'll let you arrest me and take me to jail if I can wear your trooper's hat on the way down there."

This brought an audible gasp from the other three troopers, who probably put their hands on their hats just out of instinct. Keep in mind that an Alabama state trooper's hat is as close to being God's hat as the Pope's. They don't take their hats off for anyone or let anyone touch their hats. The senior trooper said, "Fine. Here you go," and he walked over to the man and gave him his hat. The giant put on the trooper's hat, submitted to being handcuffed (it took two sets, chained together), got in the back of the senior trooper's squad car, and wore the hat all the way to jail. At the jail, the trooper retrieved his hat, booked the man with the deputies, and went back to work.

Let's review the Verbal Judo themes again to see if the senior trooper followed all of the elements: He listened to the man, who was clearly upset. He was empathetic, even though he didn't agree with the other man's perspective. He helped him save face by offering him a solution that was acceptable to both sides; and he certainly was creative in his effort to meet his goal of a safe trip to jail for all sides.

A useful part of Thompson's Verbal Judo concept is his model called LEAPS: Listen, Empathize, Ask, Paraphrase, Summarize. Let's look at each of these in more detail:

- **Listen actively.** Make eye contact, nod at the right times, and say validating things like, "I see … Okay … Tell me more …" Active listening means no multitasking, no looking at your computer (or your cell phone) when the patron is talking.

- **Empathize.** This concept is differs from being *sympathetic*. Empathy means you can "feel the other person's pain," to paraphrase Mr. Clinton, who is probably our most empathetic president since Mr. Lincoln. Sympathy means you are as emotionally involved as the other person in the issue. This too-deep perspective can cause you to get distracted and lose focus. As an example, I am empathetic about the homeless issue in this country; I don't like to see people sleeping on the streets of any US city. But I'm not so overly sympathetic that I become tearful and lose my perspective about some of the root causes of homelessness, which, in my experience, tend to be driven by the self-destructive behaviors of many of the homeless I have encountered.

- **Ask questions.** Here, you ask more open-ended questions—who, when, where, why, and how types of questions—of the other person at the beginning to get him or her to tell you more about what he or she needs. Once you've (at least) tried to get more information, you can switch over to closed-ended, yes-or-no questions to bring closure to the conversation.

- **Paraphrase.** One of the hallmarks to active listening is your ability to paraphrase what you believe the other person has said. This builds empathy and allows the other person either to correct you or to agree (if not aloud, then at least inside his or her own mind) that you heard what he or she said. This is the gateway to real understanding.

- **Summarize.** Your concluding conversations with a patron can cover what was said, what you said you would do, and, hopefully, what that person has agreed to do. Sometimes you can walk and talk as the patron heads to the exit door, having agreed to leave, somewhat cooperatively we hope, after acting out. Another alternative might be to have the patron agree to stop certain behaviors in order to be able to stay.

Best Practices Communication Tools: Some Fine Points

In Chapter 2, I discussed the need to avoid the fourth of my dad Karl Albrecht's list of the Seven Service Sins, condescension. Here are just a few phrases to avoid—unless you want to keep making things worse for yourself with the patron. These don't help the communication process, and they rarely work to gain compliance or understanding:

"You need to calm down, sir!"

"I don't care if your taxes pay my salary!"

"That's not our policy."

"That's not my department [or area]. Ask someone at the circulation desk."

"I can't authorize that unless my supervisor is here, and she's at lunch."

"What *you* need to understand, pal, is…"

"Can't you see I'm busy [or on the phone]?"

"I can't help you. I don't know who can. Good luck with that."

"I'm already late for my break. You'll have to call or come back later."

"You didn't read the instructions or directions, now did you, ma'am?"

Conversely, these phrases tend to work well with most patrons in general, and especially with those who are angry or entitled:

"You can't do that if you want to stay here."

"I can see you're upset."

"I'm sorry that happened. Let's make sure that won't happen to you again."

"Please know I'm not trying to make you mad."

"You could be right."

"It's not me; it's the computer."

"Please help me do my job for you…"

"You'll have to leave for the day…"

"Let me get your name and number and get right back to you…"

"I can get my supervisor if you'd like…"

"I can take your name and cell phone number for my supervisor if you'd like…"

As an important side note, don't rush to get your boss just because the conversation with the patron has turned difficult. Stay with it; use your communication tools and skills to work toward a successful outcome. Get your boss only after you've tried your best to handle the situation and the patron clearly wants no more part of you.

Two more ways to get more compliance with angry or entitled patrons involve semantic shifts on your part. One technique can plant the seeds for their cooperation when you say, "If I can do [something positive] for you, then will you do [something positive] for me?" Conversely, you can turn it around and say, "If you don't do [something positive] for me, then I won't be able to do [something positive] for you." Some examples: "If you can wait for me over there, then I'll be right back over to you when I'm finished looking into your request" or "If you don't stop screaming, I can't understand you, and if I can't understand you, I won't be able to help you." In other words, "Do something good for me [and comply], and I'll probably be able to do something good for you" or "If you won't cooperate, I won't be able to help you." We feed five-ton killer whales lots of tasty fish when they do what we want and nothing when they don't.

The other technique is called "thought stopping," and it's a high-risk move because when it works, it's perfect, and when it doesn't, it can make the situation instantly worse. Remember the discussion in Chapter 4 where I defined the broken-record flaw that some patrons have called persevera-tion? Their record needle is stuck on the same song or the same idea, and they can't let it go. For thought stopping, as the patron is ranting in front of you about the same issue, verse eleven, break eye contact and look around him or her for a moment and say something absolutely, completely off the topic: "Is that your red car double-parked outside?" "Is it starting to rain?" "Did I just see a stray cat try to come in here?" An off-subject question will stop perseverators dead in their tracks and bring them crashing back to real-ity in a hurry. They often say, "Huh?" or "What's that?" or "Oh, uh, where was I?," and at that point, you can swiftly move back into the conversation and take control using some closure solutions that can finally end this non-stop verbal loop. Here are two of my favorite examples of this technique.

When I was in the police academy (a brief thirty years ago), one of the human communications instructors relayed a story about the time he stopped a car during patrol late one night. The driver jumped out of his car, ran back toward this officer, and said, "I'm gonna kick your ass!" Without missing a beat, the cop said, "Hey! It's a good thing I'm into that!" The guy, now completely flustered and off balance, said, "Uh, what?" The cop said, "Stand over there until I tell you to move." "Yes, sir," said the suddenly con-fused guy, as his whole plan slipped away.

One of the movies on my Top Ten COAT (Comedies of All Time) list is Mel Brooks's *Young Frankenstein*. In the film, there's a scene where mad scientist Dr. Frankenstein (played so artfully by Gene Wilder) is locked in a cell with the Monster (the late, great Peter Boyle). As the Monster breaks his chains and prepares to grab him, Wilder says, "Hello, handsome! You're a good-looking fellow. Do you know that?" Boyle stopped and looked all around and behind him as if to say, "Who is he talking about?"

Both the cop and Gene Wilder exhibited great examples of thought stopping, which is literally what they did in both situations. When it works—and it often does, except with fall-down drunks and the psychoti-cally mentally ill—thought stopping can get the patron back on this planet and in a hurry, albeit slightly confused. It's certainly worth a test the next time you're facing a Perseverating Patron.

Reading Dangerous Faces

In his insightful book *Blink: The Power of Thinking without Thinking* (Little, Brown, 2005), Malcolm Gladwell writes about the pioneering work on face reading of UC San Francisco psychologist Dr. Paul Ekman, long known for his contributions in lie detection and the influence of body language and nonverbal behaviors. Ekman and several colleagues created the Facial Action Coding System (FACS), which identifies facial expressions created by slight shifts in the muscles of the face. These "micro expressions," or subtle changes in a person's facial features, especially under the stress of the moment, became clearer to Ekman and his team as they studied how and why someone would say one thing and then do another or appear neutral and then lash out.

As far back as 1967, Ekman and his colleague Wallace Friesen looked at how certain suicidal patients were able to convince their clinicians that they were not going to harm themselves just prior to attempting to take their own lives. By reviewing films of the interviews at slow speeds, they identified certain facial expressions that foreshadowed negative feelings the patients were trying to hide. Ekman's field work around the world in urban, rural, remote, and even primitive locations led him to conclude that all people on the planet, regardless of age, social status, gender, or intellect, express these seven basic human emotions: Anger, surprise, fear, disgust, contempt, happiness, and sadness.

Ekman's micro expressions training programs use videos that very briefly show one of these seven basic emotions on a person's face (almost faster than you can observe it; blink and you'll miss it), and you have to assess and then choose which one of the seven you saw. When you look at each of these seven human emotions, happiness, sadness, surprise, and fear are usually easy to spot. The others, anger, disgust, and contempt, can be more subtle, which makes them more difficult to read, especially when those true feelings are submerged behind the mask of a seemingly neutral face. The value of Ekman's micro expressions training is in helping participants to see the slight shifts in a facial muscle that mean something: The downward curving shape of the mouth that suggests contempt, the crinkle of the nose between the eyes that means disgust, and the brief display of teeth that suggests a raging anger being held in check.

From a threat assessment perspective, I find these visual clues to be invaluable when talking with a subject who has made threats in the past but whose emotions now are much more subterranean. They might appear to be relatively calm and collected in front of me, but I know to look harder at what I see in their faces because the truth may appear only for a second. The front stage shows us what we see; the backstage can provide us with the reasons for what we see. If you've ever had an argument with someone at home or work who said, "Whatever" or "It's fine," and you suddenly realized from looking at the person's face that it's not over or it's really not fine, then you have successfully read one of Ekman's negative micro expressions.

Eight Tools for Workplace Violence Prevention

The ideas presented here, when used effectively and early enough, can help library directors, managers, supervisors, and their stakeholders from HR as well as the city attorney or county counsel and law enforcement to intervene in cases involving threats from people inside or outside the library facility.

Constant Security/Access Control Improvements

Many big and expensive security changes are made in the aftermath of an incident. Instead, we need to be better at making smaller improvements over time. It's not necessarily the installation of a $50,000, closed-circuit television system that will keep the library safe; it's often more about making sure that all of the key card readers work and reminding employees not to prop open the back doors. Small changes and security upgrades over time can be easier for senior management to swallow and can reinforce the idea that a protection mind-set is always in place.

A Security Culture Driven by Employees

Every employee should feel like he or she is in charge of keeping the facility safe. There should be visible rewards (public praise, time off, gift cards) for employees who report physical security issues that need fixing. There should be support of and an immediate response to employees who report patron behavioral problems, threats, or criminal activities involving coworkers, patrons, ex–domestic partners, or strangers. If an employee ever says, "I knew about his disturbing comments before the shooting, but I didn't know who to tell," then you have failed to create a "courage culture," where they know who to talk to and when to speak up, both with and in confidence.

High-Risk Customer Service Training

Employees who deal with angry patrons should know how to set personal and professional boundaries (e.g., not allowing angry callers to swear at them), how to use high-stress communication tools to deescalate people who will not listen, how to change the ratios of confrontation by bringing in more help from other library staff or supervisors, and when and how to report security problems.

Identifying Hunters and Howlers

Refer back to Chapter 5's discussion of Hunter behavior versus Howler behavior. The good news is that most of the people we deal with in libraries are Howlers. They draw attention to themselves and we can manage their behaviors by setting boundaries, including those which involve locked doors and jail bars created by the police and sheriff. The bad news is that Hunters work by stealth and unless they leak information about their future plans, they are hard to identify until they act.

Consequence-Based Thinking

There must be consequences for patron behaviors that put library staff at risk. The library director, the city or county HR department, and the municipal attorneys can do their parts by working together to craft effective and updated policies and codes of conduct; supporting library department heads and frontline supervisors as they help their staff enforce consequences; and reminding all employees to be firm, fair, consistent, and assertive when dealing with problem patrons.

Threat Assessment Teams

The key to success when responding to any threat of workplace violence is the use of a Threat Assessment Team (TAT). By gathering the safety and security stakeholders into a room or via a conference call, you can come up with a viable plan in a short time span. These core stakeholders can include representatives from the library, the personnel department, the chief administrator's or the city manager's office, the police or sheriff's department; the risk management or safety officer, a behavioral health consultant, the EAP provider, outside mental health professionals, and/or threat management consultants; and, if applicable, the employee union representatives, facility directors, or an employee's direct supervisor. Everybody doesn't need to attend the entire meeting. Some people can come in, provide a key piece of information, and leave, and then the core TAT can take all the pieces of gathered knowledge about the person or incident to create a list of potential solutions.

Using Safe Rooms and Evacuation Drills (Run. Hide. Fight.)

After the use of TATs, the next best response to the threat of an active shooter is to evacuate (Run) or go to a safe room (Hide), using a "shelter in place" protocol, and wait for the police response, or defend yourself (Fight) (see the final section of this chapter for more on these three responses). The use of safe rooms in school shootings and workplace violence incidents has saved lives, with the caveat that this is not a perfect solution to the homicidal intent of a perpetrator. Safe rooms could include a break room, restroom, training classroom, conference room, supervisor's office, storage closet, or any other (preferably windowless) room that can be locked or barricaded.

Courageous Management

All of the previous seven tools are useless without this last one. Library leaders and city leaders, department heads, and frontline supervisors all need to exhibit courage and respond to any potential workplace violence threat involving patrons or employees. There is a tendency in these cases to "wish it away" and hope that inaction will lead to a solution.

We aren't trying to create a nation of tattle-tale employees. We aren't trying to turn our workspaces into locked-down prison camps. We are trying to be responsive to potential behavioral, HR, and security situations that may put the library organization at risk.

The Truth behind the Debate over "Run. Hide. Fight." with Active Shooters

In an absolute worst-case situation, where your facility is faced with the horrific possibility of a person with a gun on the premises who is intent on shooting people, you have three distinct choices: Run. Hide. Fight.

The video *Run. Hide. Fight. Surviving an Active Shooter Event*, created by the City of Houston, Texas, and the Department of Homeland Security, has had to date over 3 million YouTube views. This suggests that a lot of folks have taken the time to watch the six-minute program that now serves as the national protocol on what to do when an armed perpetrator enters a public or private business with the intent to kill.

The good news is that since the 1990s, the number of people killed in workplace violence incidents has fallen, and rather dramatically, from about 1,500 some twenty years ago to around 500 now. One death at work, for any reason, is too many, but the decline in numbers suggests that training, awareness (most of it driven by media coverage of workplace shootings), and new evacuation and police protocols are making a big difference. The *Run. Hide. Fight.* video is one of many training responses from agencies in the US government tasked with keeping employees safe, including OSHA, the Department of Labor, and the FBI, which often investigates workplace, school, and college and university shootings as part of the response and reporting work done by its Behavior Analysis Unit 2.

We learn our lessons about how to stop active shooters in our schools and workplaces mostly the hard way. The usual police tactical response right up until the 1999 Columbine High School shootings was to surround the building and wait for the arrival of the SWAT team. This approach failed that day as officers on the perimeter had to hear the anguished screams from teachers and students inside while they waited helplessly outside. From that day forward, law enforcement said, "No more!" and altered their tactics and training. When these incidents happen today, officers and deputies arrive quickly, grab their long rifles, form a fast entry plan, and go inside in teams of two to six, with the intent of engaging and stopping the shooter. As I say to employees in my training programs on this issue just before I show the *Run. Hide. Fight.* video, "And you don't want to be anywhere in the area when the cops arrive."

In essence, the "Run. Hide. Fight." response and the accompanying video present a simple concept: Vote with your feet. If you can get out of the building safely, avoiding an armed assailant and not hurting yourself in the process (sprained ankle, a fall down the stairs, etc.), then run out and away as fast as you can. Take as many people with you as is safe, avoid going to any of the usual "staging areas" (e.g., parking lots, open concourses) like you'd do for a fire drill or a gas leak, and call 911 when it's safe to do so.

The hide part is a bit tougher but just as life-saving: Leave your desk or work area, leave your stuff except for your cell phone, and run to the nearest safe room in your building. Once inside, with as many people as will fit, lock the door, barricade it with whatever heavy objects you can find, stay out of the door frame, and have people spread out inside the room, stay low, and be quiet. If you can call 911 from this position without making noise, do it. The safe room is not a bulletproof chamber; it's a break room, restroom, locker room, storage closet, utility room, training room, or supervisor's office that can be locked, preferably without windows and off the main hallway where the shooter may pass. The purpose of hiding in the safe room is to keep you and others barricaded and out of sight until the police can arrive to engage with the person with the gun(s).

The third response, fight back, is the least palatable but may be necessary to keep you and your colleagues alive. Almost any room in an office building, store, church, or factory will have something in it that you can use for protection: A fire extinguisher (for spraying or head-bashing or both), chairs, tools, desktop objects, or even heavy books. Brave and heroic people have done extraordinary things when faced with real chance-of-death events involving a shooter who has breached the safe room. Many people who had never seen themselves as capable of protecting themselves or others with force have done so when called upon and saved lives.

At this point, as President Obama likes to say, "Let me be clear." We *do not* teach the three steps of the "Run. Hide. Fight." concept to kids in K–12 schools. We certainly teach them the run and hide parts, following the directions of their teachers or other qualified adults on campus, to help them evacuate safely or shelter in place (most often in their locked classrooms), until the police arrive to engage the shooter. We don't suggest that grade school children fight perpetrators with guns. The adults on school campuses, however, have fought back and saved lives, so the concept does apply to them as employees.

Critics of the "Run. Hide. Fight." concept, and there are a vocal few, suggest that each of the three steps has its flaws. They say, "Don't leave a safe place in the building to run into harm's way! You could be much safer staying where you are and not encountering the shooter in a hallway as you try to evacuate." Or they say, "Don't run and hurt yourself as you flee! That would only make it easier for the shooter to get you." They don't like the shelter-in-place idea either: "Don't stay in one room like a sitting duck! You could get killed in there! Get out of the building!" Finally, they say, "Most people aren't trained in self-defense techniques. Fighting back could get you killed!"

To all this I say, "Run when it's safe to run. Hide where it's safe to hide. Fight if you or others around you have no other options." These may not be perfect solutions, but under the stress of these intensely frightening events, would you be able to remember to do ten things or only three? We're simply asking all employees to remember the steps—Run. Hide. Fight.—in that order, should the rare but catastrophic event of an active shooter occur. Millions of employees in this country will go through their entire careers without ever encountering an active shooter in their workplace. A small number might. The concept was designed for all, to save the few who may need it.

Your homework today is to watch the *Run. Hide. Fight.* video on YouTube (www.youtube.com/watch?v=5VcSwejU2D0). Make your own decision about whether you think the concept will work for you. If you haven't yet seen this video, one caveat: The shooter (who's bald, dressed all in black, and looks like the action movie actor Vin Diesel) enters the building and starts blasting people with a shotgun quite quickly. You don't see any blood, but it's still alarming to see him shooting people. When I show the video in my training classes, I skip ahead to the 1:30 mark, to avoid triggering traumatic responses in people who may have been in a critical incident before and don't want to reexperience it. You can watch the whole thing or skip ahead; either way, the description of the method is the same.

Until active shooters stop their attacks (not likely, especially as we consider the increasing movements of international terrorists back to our shores) or someone comes up with a better plan that doesn't involve eleven steps and issuing everyone ballistic vests, I vote for "Run. Hide. Fight."

★ CHAPTER 7

Conducting Your Own Site Security Survey

In life and work, is it better to know or not know? Some surprises are fun; others not so much. This issue arises whenever I assess the state of a library's facility security. Too often at libraries, the city manager or the chief administrative officer and his or her city attorney or county counsel become afraid that any noted security gaps somehow raise their liability and "put them on notice" to make immediate and costly security changes. Less often, these fears of knowing too much about pressing safety or security needs come from the library director, who is anxious about the impact on his or her budget. And in an interesting twist, often the most *public* support for making security improvements at the library comes from the area's elected officials (library patrons and library employees vote, after all). Now, getting those same seemingly gung-ho city council members or board of supervisors to come up with the necessary funds to implement the security improvements they felt so strongly about when talking with the media and the public, well, that's when the *private* discussions start about how tight the budget suddenly appears to be.

The good news is that knowing what needs to be addressed in your library can help lessen your liability by being able to make ongoing changes as time and budgets allow. Most security improvements can be initiated over time, unless, of course, the security concern is absolutely flagrant (we can't lock the bloody doors to the building tonight because the locks are all damaged), in which case emergency funds must be tapped and prompt actions taken. The bad news is that every day any public facility opens its doors, it's already at 100 percent liability anyway. On average, Disneyland in Los Angeles or Disney World in Orlando has one serious injury accident that requires an ambulance every single day. That doesn't stop the Magic Kingdom from operating on both coasts, rain or shine.

The other good news about the results of a site security survey for a library facility (at least the type I create, hopefully along with my like-minded budget-sensitive colleagues) is that many security deficiencies can be solved by policy changes, employee reminders or fresh training, or simple solutions, like keeping certain doors locked at all times. As we create these reports, we try to keep the costs in mind, knowing how difficult it is to get city councils and county boards to spend money on capital improvements (e.g., knocking down walls, pulling wires through drop ceilings, buying expensive electronic equipment), until, of course, there is a significant security incident, and then the money often magically appears from somewhere. Such "event-driven thinking" is both common and not useful, as it's reactionary and doesn't consider that the world is becoming more unpredictable, more insecure, and more unsecured.

At the risk of putting myself out of a job, this chapter discusses the process you can follow at your library to conduct a full facility security assessment; create a Site Security Survey Report for your leadership team, library board, elected officials, city manager, county administrator or chief executive officer to follow; and help those stakeholders and your employees implement the changes you have suggested.

Step 1: Start with a Library Employee Security Survey

Before beginning your facility's physical security improvements, it makes sense to first ask employees what they think about where they work. For many reasons, all of which are difficult for me to understand, employee opinion surveys are as rare as leprechauns riding unicorns to the pot of gold at the end of a double rainbow; companies and government agencies just don't do them. As painful as the answers can be, when it comes to library security, it's better to ask the questions so you know in advance what to expect, what to prepare for, and how to do it. If this is true, then why do so few library organizations conduct security-related employee surveys to gauge the perceptions of the level of safety at their facilities? Can we agree that we need to ask our employees what is safe or not safe at their library facilities, and do it on a regular basis (like every few years)?

Critics of security-related surveys say that once they get the information, the organization or the facility somehow starts a "liability clock," meaning they will have to take immediate steps to correct every single deficiency before they can open the doors again. This is an overreaction. The truth is that every public facility is already at a high watermark for liability anyway. We will always be questioned by outsiders as to the safety and security of our entire library building, from slip and falls in a wet restroom to an attack against a patron by a mentally ill homeless person.

The value of starting with a safety and security survey questionnaire is twofold: It gives every employee who participates a voice in his or her own well-being at work, and it gives management a road map to make cost-effective, reasonable, and necessary physical security or security policy changes by prioritizing the answers received. Related to the first point, we know some employees want to be heard and need a staff forum for their concerns (your more vocal employees, who will bring up security issues and problematic patrons during staff meetings, often more than a bit loudly), but others would rather remain anonymous. Administering a survey gives both groups their chance to be heard, on paper. As for the second point, we don't have to make every fix suggested, but we can certainly demonstrate to the employees and others (library boards, city or county elected officials, and even plaintiff's attorneys) that we are taking new steps to minimize security risks and maximize staff and patron safety.

What follows is an eleven-question survey that poses tough questions to library staff members, with the intent of discovering what they may want to say about security, but perhaps not out loud to their supervisors, through an anonymous forum. Consider using the following survey for your facilities. You can modify these questions (just a bit) to fit your specific organization, but be careful not to change the meaning too much because you are wary of the answers. You should tell all staff that your process will be to gather their opinions, analyze and prioritize their concerns with the senior library staff, give them an overview of what you heard from them, and then discuss what you plan to do going forward. You can print out a version of the following questionnaire to distribute, create an online portal on your intranet, or have employees complete this survey online using free survey software like SurveyMonkey (www.surveymonkey.com) or something similar.

All of the employees who participate in the survey process will want to know that their opinions were heard, valued, and acted on. People need closure from these exercises, so be sure to build a recap discussion into the project. It's not about overpromising or keeping the results secret; it's about keeping your staff apprised and updated so you can share the message that we're all in charge of security at our libraries. Here's one example of the library employee security questionnaire:

Library Employee Security Survey

This survey will help us conduct a risk management, safety, and security assessment of our library facilities. Your answers are anonymous. We want your opinions, not your name. We will share the results at a later staff meeting.

Library Branch: _____

Employee Type (check only one):

    Full-time staff   _____
    Part-time staff   _____
    Supervisor   _____

Please circle your best answer for each of the following questions.

1. How would you describe your Library's current Code of Patron Conduct?

    a. Don't have one or don't know if we have one
    b. Needs improvement
    c. Adequate
    d. Excellent

2. To keep staff and patrons safe, which of the following would you say your Library has?

    a. No security policies and procedures
    b. Poor security policies and procedures
    c. Adequate security policies and procedures
    d. Excellent security policies and procedures

---

3. How would you describe yourself on most days, as you deal with all types of patrons?

    a. Not afraid of any patrons
    b. Somewhat afraid of some patrons
    c. Afraid of some patrons
    d. Very afraid of some patrons

4. How would you rate the level of support you receive from supervisors when dealing with challenging patrons?

    a. No support
    b. Needs improvement
    c. Adequate
    d. Excellent

5. How would you describe your Library's relationship with the police, in terms of visibility and response?

    a. No relationship
    b. Needs improvement
    c. Adequate
    d. Excellent

6. How would you rate your Library's emergency evacuation plan for patrons and staff?

    a. Don't have one or don't know if we have one
    b. Needs improvement
    c. Adequate
    d. Excellent

7. How would you rate the number of lockdown or shelter-in-place drills done at your Library?

    a. Don't do them or don't know if we do them
    b. Needs improvement
    c. Adequate
    d. Excellent

8. In the rare event of an active shooter situation in your Library, you are familiar with the concept of "Run. Hide. Fight."

    a. True
    b. False

9. If you were ever concerned about a troubled coworker (who is depressed, hostile, bullying, threatening, etc.), how would you rate the HR services that could be provided for that coworker?

    a. No services
    b. Needs improvement
    c. Adequate
    d. Excellent

10. How would you describe the availability of community or social services (e.g., homeless outreach, churches, charities, elder care, mental health support) near your facility to help with challenging patrons?

    a. Don't know about such services
    b. No services
    c. Needs improvement
    d. Adequate
    e. Excellent

11. Please add any additional comments about facility security below:

_____

_____

_____

_____

_____

_____

Let's interpret some possible results. Timing in life is everything. Unless the work culture at the library is crushingly toxic or you conduct the survey in the aftermath of a serious incident during which staff were injured or worse, you can probably predict the totality of answers before you even give out the survey. I'm hardly a stat head (I did poorly in the grad school class known accurately as "Sadistics"), but most of the survey responses I tend to see fall along the usual Gaussian bell curve: 15 percent of employees love the library, no matter what we do; 15 percent of employees hate the library, no matter what we do; 60 percent of the people feel mostly good about the library; and 10 percent have no opinion. And although I find the responses to the first ten survey questions to be interesting, I find the comments solicited from question 11 to be fascinating. You don't have to address every single comment, but this section is often where the biggest safety and security challenges come from, as do some good solutions.

Once you've collected the surveys and tabulated the results, you can review the totality of the information, including the comments. You should use software that is sophisticated enough to be able to pull out specific data based on the branch locations and types of employees. When crafting the final survey report based on the comments section, you may see some recurring themes (which can range from helpful to snotty to overly lengthy to odd to truly goofy, head-scratching comments like, "All staff members should be immediately trained in the martial arts, during working hours"); ignore those you deem less than useful in your final report.

Be a critical evaluator when reading the comments: Do these make sense in context? After eliminating the comments obviously designed to get a rise out of the bosses (e.g., "We need a beer keg in the employee break room"), determine what appears most commonly as a security concern. Do the comments surprise us or were we expecting some of these answers? Are the corrections we need to make more concerned with physical security changes or policy changes? What are the most critical branch-specific issues we must address? Which relationships do we need to strengthen, inside and outside the branches?

It takes thick skin to read survey data and assess their validity when it comes to your own branch. If you're in management, it's easy to get self-righteous and defensive about the employees' answers or comments or both. Saying, "They just don't understand our budget restrictions or the political environment we're working under" or "They knew this could be a hard job, involving difficult interactions with entitled patrons, when they took it" may make you feel better, but their truth is their truth and their version of reality is what it is. Wishing for more positive answers wastes the time you will need to apply the security solutions that can address the most prevalent employee concerns.

Your employees will want to know the results of the survey as soon as you can create a summary, but first you need to decide as a management group how much data to reveal to them. This is more about data validity and time management versus keeping secrets from the staff. My usual approach is to provide the collective answers for each question to the staff and a selected sample of the most common or most interesting comments. For example, you could create a report or a slide presentation with either the raw numbers or the percentages, as shown here:

1. How would you describe your Library's current Code of Patron Conduct?
   a. Don't have one or don't know if we have one (5 employees; 10%)
   b. Needs improvement (15 employees; 30%)
   c. Adequate (25 employees; 50%)
   d. Excellent (5 employees; 10%)

Providing the data in a report or on a screen during a staff meeting helps to give the process transparency, encourages conversation as to what conclusions might be drawn from the data, prioritizes the results into "need to do" versus "nice to do" categories, and gives the staff a realistic timeline as to when or if the changes will happen. You are neither overpromising nor underpromising; you're just reporting.

The Library Employee Security Survey Summary Report and the resulting conclusions from the Site Security Survey Report (see the following section) can also play a critical role in getting important stakeholders outside your branch to pay attention to the security concerns. Having a meeting to discuss the report results with your city manager or county administrative officer, city attorney or county counsel, or law enforcement representative can be an eye-opening experience for them. I've seen many of these folks come out of a library-related safety and security–oriented discussion with wide-eyed looks on their faces. What they previously took for granted—that the library doesn't need their attention when it comes to safety or security issues—can change to "Let's get busy on the physical security, training, or policy changes necessary to keep our employees and our patrons safer."

Step 2: Conduct a Site Security Survey of Your Library

The value of doing the employee perceptional survey about security first is that it makes it much easier to do the site security survey because the employees have told you in advance what to focus on. This can make you look like a genius because your report will address their most pressing concerns. As an example, I conducted a site security survey for a library where the employees parked across the street from the facility. Every day they had to cross an uncontrolled two-lane road where people sped by during the morning and evening rush hours. I arrived at noon to do the work, parked, and went inside. Near the end of my assessment, I sat down with several employees who told me their biggest safety concern was getting in and out of the building without being hit by a car. I had no clue this was an issue because I got there after everyone else. If I had not asked them, I would have left this out of my report. As a result, I contacted the county about the issue, they did a speed survey and installed a crosswalk and a traffic light.

Our Security Approach

Any security change—whether related to new equipment, new policies, hiring guards, or training—should be measured by three critical issues: The cost, the work culture fit, and the feasibility. Can we afford it now or later? Can we find a cost-effective way to purchase what we need by teaming up with another department, getting a grant, using a different budget, having it installed by our maintenance people, and so forth? Will it enhance our current work culture here or will it cause problems? For example, some cities and counties require their employees, including library staff, to wear visible ID cards at all times, and some cities and counties have this policy but just don't enforce it, for whatever reason. If the security improvements clash with the existing culture—"We've never done it that way here before"— then they may not be realistic solutions: "People don't like wearing IDs, and that's that." And is it feasible? Can we find an in-house resource, like the public works, maintenance, or facilities staff, to do the work or do we need to contact an outside vendor? Can we get advice from the police or sheriff's department's Crime Prevention Unit? How can we create a safer environment without running cables for expensive camera systems? If we can't afford a full-time security officer, can we at least hire a part-time guard to work on a rotating basis, with different shifts and different hours, to keep the bad guys slightly off balance? Can we get security equipment donated to the library from vendors in our community?

An important semantic note for the report: I'm not a lawyer, but I am familiar with what keeps them awake at night (besides too much coffee). I'm careful in my Site Security Survey Reports not to call the solutions I suggest "requirements" or "recommendations"—my preferred phrase is *security improvement options*—and I don't rank them in terms of importance either. (If the concern is immediate, I tell the library director it must be addressed right away, while I'm still on-site.) I've been stung on this issue before because some plaintiff's attorneys are quick to leap on the idea that if a security report calls for "recommendations" and they are not all instituted at once, that's the reason his or her client was wronged or injured: "This report gave you one hundred recommendations and you only competed ninety-nine of them; therefore, that missing one was the reason my client suffered." The phrase *security improvement options* at least gives the library some flexibility as to which fixes they complete, why, and when, using the tripod formula of Cost, Culture, and Feasibility.

Thinking about Your SCIFs

What is the one room or the one system in your library that is the most critical, the one that if it was compromised or it failed, the results would be catastrophic? If there was a fire, a flood, a data breach or hacking, or data was destroyed, what would be the negative impact on your library? In the answers to these questions lies the security concept known as "protecting the SCIFs," or Sensitive Compartmented Information Facilities. The US government, the Central Intelligence Agency, the National Security Agency, the military, and the Department of Defense and many of its contractors all use SCIFs, which are specially secured rooms, or entire facilities, designed and hardened to protect critical data.

While you don't need a lead-lined room and armed US Marines standing door guard at your SCIF, the concept is still useful in library security. Perhaps your SCIF is the IT server room that houses your mainframe computers, servers, and telephone lines. Maybe this room lacks sturdy door locks, a sign-in procedure, or adequate fire protection for the expensive and critical electronics. Perhaps the room includes the computer system that holds all of your patron data. If this system were hacked or failed, what would you do to restore it? Besides the employees, what are your library's most important, mission-critical, must-protect assets? What would close you down if it suffered damage?

Here's an example of SCIF use in the private sector. A company that sells sports team uniforms to high schools and colleges around the country takes all of its orders over its toll-free telephone number in June. The company spends the rest of the year designing new products and filling orders, but June is its most important month. As such, the SCIF, the most important room in the company's factory, is the room that houses the telephone system. If the phone lines go down, the company goes out of business—it's that simple—and so it protects that room with security rivaling that used by a Federal Reserve Bank. As part of your security survey, you need to identify your particular SCIF and determine if the security in place to protect it is sufficient. Of course, you should always value protecting human lives first, over equipment, but keeping your identified SCIF safe is certainly important.

Your Library Security Assessment Team

When conducting a security assessment of your library, you don't need to walk alone. It's useful to invite your security stakeholders and walk-through partners, which could include a facilities employee (to explain where the wires run and why, how to get on the roof, and where to shut off the gas, electricity, and water); a police officer or deputy or a representative from the Crime Prevention Unit (often a specially trained civilian); a representative from your city's or county's risk management department or the city or county safety officer; and/or any longtime managers or employees who have extensive knowledge of the facility.

This group should start at the outside of the facility and assess the perimeter of the building, including the patron and staff parking areas; the exterior lights; the landscaping; and the delivery areas and book drops. Moving inside, the group members can go through each room and, along the way, think like crooks: "How would I get inside this facility and what would I steal or who would I hurt once I'm inside?" Someone in this group needs to take pictures of potentially problematic areas that can be included in the report for better visual impact.

The Site Security Review Process

Here are the areas a typical site security survey can cover for a library. You can use these as subject headings for your report:

- **Security in depth:** Look at the facility from the outside, paying attention to graffiti, vandalism, transient activity, and loiterers, and then look at it from the inside, focusing on employee and patron safety.

- **Perimeter security review:** Look at the quality of the exterior lighting; the need for landscaping changes; the position and number of the bike racks; the location and security of the book depositories; the security of the warehouse doors or delivery areas; the parking areas and crosswalks; exterior exit doors and the need for improved locks or access control devices like keypads or card readers; and any existing alarm systems or cameras or the need for them. What is the "feel" you get when you look at the outside of your building? Does everything seem okay or does it need improvements?

- **Facility access control:** Do the exterior doors need new locks or gate hardware or new card readers or keypad access controls? Do employees use side or staff entrances that need new hardware? Is the signage sufficient or do patrons try to come in through staff entrances? Does the signage address no trespassing or the presence of security cameras inside the library? (Don't post signs about cameras if you don't have them or they don't work. If they don't work, remove them immediately.) Does the library have exterior cameras that cover the building perimeter and the parking lot? How would you break into this facility if you were a burglar?

HR, Security, Emergency, and Evacuation Policy and Procedure Review

Any assessment of security calls for a complete review of all policies related to protecting employees and patrons, including looking at employee HR manuals; the library's code of conduct; facility emergency plans (fire controls and alarms, water or gas leaks, electrical hazards, chemical spills); evacuation plans (fire, tornado, hurricane, snow, earthquake, active shooters); and workplace violence response plans. Are there posted sets of guidelines for employees to quickly consult in an emergency, with phone numbers and resources to call? Do your employees need to dial 911 or 9-911 to get emergency help? The following are important areas to focus on when conducting your policy and procedure review:

- **Information security:** Review all written materials related to the use and protection of your computer systems, Internet protocols, and telephone systems. Assess the state of facility security for your IT server rooms, phone rooms, and utility panels.

- **Vendor procedures:** Review the vendor protocols for your facility. Who makes deliveries or repairs and when and how do they do them? Vendors can include people who service your soda machines, bottled water dispensers, or copy machines or provide outside janitorial or landscaping services. Do these people have keys or key cards or knowledge of the alarm codes? Are they in the building when employees are not there? Have there been any incidents related to theft or misuse of phones, faxes, copy machines, postage meters, or the Internet for which a vendor is suspected?

- **Internal/external alarms:** Is there a burglar alarm for the facility? Who receives the alarm—an alarm company, the police, no one? Who from the library responds after hours if there is an open door or a true break-in? Are there panic alarms at the facility? Do they ring to an alarm company, the police, or a supervisor's office?

- **First-aid procedures:** Is there an AED in the facility? Are all staffers trained to use it? Are all staffers trained in adult, child, and infant CPR? Are there multiple first-aid kits, and do all staffers know where they are?

- **Fiduciary instrument controls:** Is there a safe or a vault at the facility? How often is the combination changed and is the combination issued on a need-to-know basis? Are the cash-handling procedures sufficient, or do they need to be updated? Who takes the money to the city or county finance department? If the cash and credit cards go to the bank, then who makes the deposits? Does he or she change the process, use a nondescript bag, and vary the driving route to the bank? Are audits done on a regular basis, including for petty cash?

- **Security guards:** Review the current posted orders and make adjustments to their job duties. Quiz the on-duty security officer about how he or she would respond to certain patron behavior scenarios or emergency situations. Meet with the security company vendor if you aren't satisfied with the officer's answers to discuss the need for more training, new posted orders, or a new guard.

- **Police and fire department interactions:** When was the last inspection by the fire marshal? Have the fire extinguishers been serviced recently? Have you asked the watch commander for your police or sheriff's department to send the beat officer or beat deputy to the library for a meet and greet? Do all staff members know that they can call the police at any time without having to ask permission? Do all staffers know whether they need to dial 911 or 9-911 to get help? Do they know to give both the facility address and the location(s) in the library with the problem? Do they know to describe behaviors instead of using labels (e.g., "Send the police right away. We have a mentally ill man threatening people." versus "There's a crazy guy in here!")? Are all employees told to fill out a Security Incident Report for any security-related incident or near incident?

- **Workplace violence response/active shooters:** Have all staffers seen the *Run. Hide. Fight.* online video, created by the Department of Homeland Security and the City of Houston, Texas? Are all staff members told to report threats of violence against them or between patrons, including bomb threats, gang threats, or domestic violence threats? Are all employees told that if they have a domestic violence–related restraining order against someone who may come to the library, they need to tell the library director so he or she can create a work safety plan and coordinate with the police, if necessary?

- **Emergency and security drills:** Does the library hold fire drills at least once per year? How about for weather-related or other natural disaster drills? Does the library practice active shooter evacuations or hold lockdown drills? (You can get good support from your fire department or local law enforcement agencies to help you do these effectively.)

Step 3: Create a Site Security Survey Report and Act on It

Once you have completed your review, write a draft report and have your HR, risk management, safety, and security stakeholders review the entire document. Add their suggestions and corrections before you turn the draft into a final report.

Implementation

The key to an effective Site Security Survey Report is to not let it die on the vine. Many such reports rest comfortably on the office bookshelves or filing cabinets of senior library or city or county management (never any of mine, of course) because although they initially might have had some real enthusiasm and desire to get the information and act on it, it is only too easy for them to get sidetracked by other, more pressing concerns. It's easy to view the report as the end of the site security assessment project; in reality, it's just the beginning. Having the data as to what needs improvement is useful; not acting on it in a timely manner devalues the report. Most security-related problems don't fix themselves, and the information gathered in March may be completely different come September. It takes effort to prioritize the findings in the report based, first, on urgency and then on the Big Three: Cost, Culture, and Feasibility. Coming up with a procedural plan that is then put into action is the key to success here. The squeaky report gets the grease.

Follow-Up

The way to keep the fruits of your labor from withering is to agree as a stakeholder group to meet at guaranteed, scheduled, and calendared intervals to discuss the next steps, what has been done, what still needs to be done, and what new information has come up that may enhance or replace what you've already discovered. Some libraries have a standing safety committee that can help keep the momentum going. But if you want to fulfill the promise you made to keep your employees safe (part of the mandate from the federal and your state OSHA's "General Duty Clause") and your patrons safe, you have to act on what you've created. The best way to defeat the efforts of plaintiff's attorneys, who want to accuse you of either doing nothing, because you have no Site Security Survey Report, or having a report but not implementing it, is to act on it, in a steady and demonstrable fashion.

When you work in harmony with your security stakeholders to make good, reasonable, and effective facility security improvements and then see them work, that's not the time to take the day off. Your reward for vigilance is—you guessed it—more vigilance.

CHAPTER 8

Community Partnerships

Law Enforcement, Mental Health, and Homeless Services

When hearing of an incident at the library that involved the police responding to arrest a particularly problematic patron of the misguided, homeless, mentally ill, drug-using, stealing, abusive, or violent variety, some of our less-than-aware citizens may ask themselves a series of (stupid) questions:

"The library? Why do homeless people go to a library?"

"What is there to steal at a library?"

"Why would someone abandon a child in a library?"

"Who brings a gun to a library?"

"Who shows up drunk at a library?"

"Who gets in a fight with a patron, and then the cops, at a library?"

If you work in a facility where all of these things have been done by all of the problematic patrons discussed in this book, you have your answer at the ready: "Because they can. The library is warm when it's cold out and cool when it's hot out. There are chairs, sofas, tables, books, magazines, bathrooms, and Internet-ready computers. We are open long hours and we cannot choose our customers. We can only respond to their behavior when it hurts our business."

You can define the arrival of the police at your facility to handle a problem patron in two ways—positively and negatively. The police are a good force multiplier because they can enforce significant consequences in ways (e.g., using handcuffs, trips to jail, citations, civil stay-away orders) that you simply can't. On the other hand, the sound of the cops jingling up to your front door, radios blaring and steely eyes at the ready, is an indicator that whatever you tried to do with the patron probably failed.

This is not to say that this is your fault. As a staff member or supervisor, you may have tried all the high-risk communication tools discussed thus far. You were empathic, a good listener, careful not to be condescending, used low tones, were respectful, protected the person's dignity, and tried to be a creative problem solver. And, yet, here are the cops and the person leaves with them in a vigorously unhappy state, possibly en route to the Gray Bar Hotel for the night or to a bed at the county mental health hospital for several hours, days, or even the two-week maximum for patients. I'm not faulting your efforts. As Teddy Roosevelt so accurately said, "Do the best you can, with what you have, where you are." I would alter his phrasing slightly to say, "Do the best you can, with *who* you have, where you are."

In other words, if we agree that a small number of challenging or problematic patrons cause the most number of problems, we need to look at *solving* their problems in ways that work for them and us. We need to bring in more help, besides just the cops, who typically take care of only our most pressing business when we need them to. It's time to get more assertive, creative, and thoughtful as to who can help make your facility safer by bringing in their respective expertise.

An example: An elderly man with significant dementia and other age-related cognitive issues came into a city library and pulled out a large butcher knife. He began waving the knife around in a way that suggested he felt he had to protect himself from whoever he believed was trying to harm him. The library staff did the right thing, isolating him from other patrons, giving him a wide berth, talking to him in careful tones from behind good proxemic barriers—all while someone else got on the horn to the police. He actually left the library before the police arrived and wandered around inside the city hall complex that included the library and the police department. The police finally arrived and carefully took him into custody without incident or injuries. (As a side note, having the police station adjacent to your library is no guarantee of a rapid response in an emergency. Most patrol cops are in the field. If your emergency happens after 4:00 or 5:00 p.m., it's unlikely any detectives or command staff are still in the police building. That's why calling 911 or 9-911 is the preferred method of contacting the police, not calling there directly and asking a records clerk working the late shift to transfer you to the dispatcher.) Once the man was in custody, he was taken by the police to the county mental health hospital for an evaluation, and the clinicians decided he needed to stay with them for a few days while they stabilized his medication.

During that time, the city activated its TAT, which consisted of trained representatives from personnel, the library, the police, the city manager's office, risk management, the city attorney, and me. We discussed what to do with or for the man and had kicked around several responses when someone (from the library, no less) said, "I know him. I think he was a veteran. Why don't we contact the local VA [Veterans Affairs] hospital to see if they can help us with him?" Cue the trumpets played by the angels. That is what we did. The VA assigned a social worker to him and was able to get him into a VA-sponsored facility that dealt with Alzheimer's patients, where he got the help he needed. Problem neatly solved. Not having been in the military myself, I never would have thought of that possible solution. It worked because the people around the table were willing to brainstorm a bit and call the people or the agency most aligned with his type of problem. Sheer genius.

With that success story in mind, let's consider the world of possible response partners for your library when it comes to dealing with a small number of patrons who can cause significant heartaches and headaches.

Working with Your Law Enforcement Partners

Liaison relationships with your local law enforcement are critical to your ongoing facility security and staff safety. The police can use their usual leverage to get unstable patrons to leave, to arrest people who show up at your facility who are disruptive, high on drugs or alcohol, or who frighten other patrons or staff. Don't discount their presence as a useful and even long-term deterrent against problem patrons who must get the message to either comply or stay away once the consequences become severe enough. (As the owner of seven dogs, I know that imposing no consequences for negative behaviors means that those behaviors will only either continue or escalate.)

Some library staff have the perspective that they are somehow bothering the police by calling them, especially for what appears to be low-level issues like the homeless pestering patrons by asking them for money or mentally ill people sleeping in the bathrooms. Put simply, the function of the police in our society is not to fight crime but to "keep the peace." When I worked for the San Diego Police Department, the motto painted on the side of our patrol cars (besides "America's Finest City," which is a never-ending source of debate with every other Chamber of Commerce in the United States) was "To Protect and Serve." True, these are the functions of every law enforcement agency, large or small. But in the old days, the San Diego PD car-side motto was "Your Safety Is Our Business," which I think captures the spirit of what the cops are supposed to do in our cities and, more specifically, in our libraries.

In my Perfect Library World, you would see a cop or a sheriff's deputy from your city or county come by your library every few days, on an irregular basis. Every library facility is on the beat of some officer or deputy who has the duty to make sure things stay safe and secure there, as with every other private or public business. But there should be even more of a bond here with the law enforcement officer who has beat responsibility for your branch. Not just technically speaking, but literally speaking, you are both employees of the same entity. County sheriffs should protect county libraries and their employees, who are county workers too, just like city police officers should protect city library employees.

Back in my Perfect Library World, a cop would come through your library once per day for a few days, twice a day for a few days, and then not again for a few days, during the week and on weekends. He or she would say hello, check the stacks and the floor, pop into the restrooms, and stop for a chat with you or any other employee or supervisor, just to make sure things are all right in the library for that moment. The point to these random patrols is to keep the potential or actual crooks, thieves, drunks, gang members, drug dealers, and so on, who may frequent your library on their toes. They should have to guess when the cops will be there.

Yes, the cops are busy in your town and mine. When I was with the San Diego PD, we had 2,000 officers. We have about 1,635 now, depending on whether you believe the different figures coming from the mayor's office, the chief's office, or the Police Officers Association. Most law enforcement agencies are shorthanded. Depending on the numbers you look at—and why they can't come up with an accurate figure continues to baffle me—the total number of cops in the United States is just under 700,000. All of them have to protect a lot of land and more than 300 million people—no easy chore, to be sure. Despite these alarming numbers, they still have a responsibility to protect and serve, and it's my belief that you should push your needs for facility security and staff and patron safety higher up on their current list of daily duties.

Part of getting an improved police response comes from understanding a few things about the police culture. Cops don't go where they don't feel welcome (since a lot of people really, really hate them anyway), so they won't come to your facility, unless it's an emergency/911 call, if the management or staffers treat them like dog poop on the nice carpet when they arrive. You don't have to agree with their approach to crime, their community relations efforts (or the lack thereof), or their quasi-military approach to things (uniforms, ranks, high and tight haircuts, muscles, hats, sunglasses, loud radios, etc.), but you should see them as fellow humans who have a difficult job and who took that difficult job because they counterintuitively move toward danger and away from safety.

As such, cops are highly sensitive to their environments. If your library has a clean and safe employees-only restroom for them to use (Priority #1), a place in the back office where they can sit and drink a cup of coffee and catch up on their reports (Priority #2), and an atmosphere where they feel welcomed and appreciated (actually, the real Priority #1), then they will frequent your facility. Don't worry that they will be hanging around the back all day, just chatting and sitting around. They may sit in your employees-only area just long enough to eat their lunch and finish a report before they have to go back out to face another barrage of radio calls. You and they both should want this type of "customer closeness."

Often the best way to get the police to start scheduling at least irregular visits to your branch is to call the Watch Commander's Office and ask the supervisor there if you can set up a meeting with the beat officer or beat deputy who has responsibility for your facility. You can start these meet and greets on the right foot by simply introducing yourself and your staff and asking if the officer or deputy can come by to check on the library from time to time. You can discreetly point out or quietly discuss certain problem patrons—people the officer or deputy may know on a first-name basis any-way—and ask if you can call his or her cell phone number for a nonemergency situation where a police presence would help quiet things down.

Most officers and deputies understand the concept of escalation and the use of problem-oriented policing as they fit your context. They know the Pareto principle as it applies to crime—20 percent of the crooks commit 80 percent of the crimes—and that a small number of irritating ne'er-do-wells create most of the petty but irritating "social fabric" crimes in and around your facility. They are well aware that if they can spend some time and energy on targeting certain highly problematic street people, like the untreated mentally ill or drug-using thieves, then they can dramatically and directly impact the quality of life in a neighborhood.

Here's an example of problem-oriented policing: Police know that drug users steal and commit burglaries to fund their devastating habits. A heroin user with a $100-per-day habit will have to steal $1,000 worth of your and my stuff to take to a shady pawn shop, since he usually only gets ten cents on the dollar. Locking up this one guy can save his neighborhood about $365,000 per year in stolen merchandise. Don't believe me? Let's do some Heroin Math: A habit costing $100 per day means $1,000 per day of stolen goods multiplied by 365 days. Therefore, catching this one guy becomes a priority for the local police because they know how much of a negative impact he has on the community every day he is free to roam and use drugs and steal.

If I know my problematic and criminally motivated library patrons as I like to think I do, I'm ready to bet big that 80 percent of your patron conduct problems that could or should involve the police coming to your facility are perpetrated by 20 percent of the people you encounter each day. In other words, it's the same small number of people creating the same large number of incidents, over and over again. Your local cops should be willing to step in and enforce consequences. Your first call to the Watch Commander's Office can start that important discussion process.

And, as in all things bureaucratic, you know the squeaky phone call gets the grease. If contacting the watch commander has not led to a meeting with your beat officer or beat deputy, start working your way up the chain of command until you get to captains, commanders, deputy chiefs, assistant chiefs, or the chief's office at the police department or the same, plus the undersheriff or the sheriff at the sheriff's department.

Working with Your Community Partners

Since you are a public agency providing a needed public service, it makes sense to go to other public service agencies when you need help with some more difficult members of that public. And besides the host of available city or county social service departments that can provide information, support, or intervention, many private-sector, quasi-government, or grant-funded groups can help with their own brand of expertise.

Previous chapters described the most challenging patrons as being the entitled, the angry, the young, the old, the mentally ill, and the substance abuser. There's an agency, a community group, or an association for all of them. When I speak to library people about calling in or calling on outside help, I hear a host of excuses and rationalizations as why that won't work: "We tried to call them and they never responded." "We don't know who to speak to over there." "They said they couldn't help or that they wanted to help but were just too busy." When I hear these reasons, I say this, with love in my heart, "Try harder."

And while nongovernmental outside agencies or private-sector providers, such as church groups, the Salvation Army, grant-funded substance abuse programs, and the like, are under no obligation to help their friends at the library, that's not always true for your fellow city or county compadres who provide behavioral health or social services. They may say they are too busy to help, but a well-placed phone call from an irritated and insistent city manager or chief administrative officer on your behalf can help them see the wisdom of across-the-hall, all-paid-by-the-same-municipality cooperation.

Homeless Advocacy Groups

Every downtown or urban part of every midsized to large city in this country has a homeless problem. The complexity of this issue makes it hard to ever solve it completely. There are a number of paradoxical realities to the problem, starting with the fact that some men like living on the streets (no woman with a child ever wants to be homeless, and the fear of sexual assault for homeless women and children is a cold reality). The men on the streets who avoid shelters (too many rules to follow, you can't smoke inside, and you have to stay sober when you're there) and substance abuse treatment programs say they like being free, getting loaded, not being subject to rules or boundaries, and being able to do and say whatever or go wherever they want. I've talked to a lot of these gents, and I'm not sure they sing the same song when it's twelve degrees outside, but when the weather is fine, they often like their situation.

I've also met with mental health clinicians who work with this high-risk population who tell me the same; these people want to be left alone, they want physical space, and they want to be able to get drunk or high. Because so many of the longtime homeless have some form of mental illness and/ or an ongoing substance abuse problem, topped off by a number of chronic medical issues, it's hard to know what to tackle first. From a safety perspective, when dealing with homeless people in the library, recall from previous chapters that you need to use proxemic barriers like space and distance, avoid touching them or their stuff, and treat them with empathy and dignity.

One of the benefits of your library's establishing an ongoing working relationship with one or more homeless advocacy groups from local government or the private sector is that they can attack the issue in ways you cannot. Homeless people benefit from day lockers to store their belongings, shower facilities, access to clean clothes, meals, haircuts, bus tokens, help filling out job applications, and services like Legal Aid to help with their problems related to court appearances, citations, warrants, child support, and the like. These are specific, useful services that homeless advocacy organizations can provide, straight to their clients, and as such, they can give you various informational resources to give out to the homeless people who frequent your library.

These relationships and the often-hidden resources that may be available all start with a dialogue between you and as many advocacy groups as you can contact. I realize you already have a full-time job at the library, but if you consider the time, energy, and stress that you and your colleagues spend dealing with the homeless population, the more help you get from people and groups who have spent their careers tackling these problems, the more you can feel like you can take back control of your facility.

We know not all homeless outreach is provided by the local government. As an example, in my city of San Diego, the Alpha Project is a nonprofit entity that specializes in getting homeless people off the streets, into shelters, and into treatment programs. They drive around in vans and coax homeless people who are truly ready for treatment to come in and get enrolled in a recovery program.

The San Diego Police Department has both the PERT, which stands for Psychiatric Emergency Response Team, and the HOT, or Homeless Outreach Team. These are squads of specially trained cops who partner with mental health clinicians and social workers in the field—they actually ride along together—to contact and try to address the problems of people with severe mental illness, substance abuse, homelessness, and other significant life–coping skills problems. The goal is not jail, but support, treatment, and patience for a collection of people who often take one step forward and away from their issues only to then take seven steps right back.

Consider how you might contact these support agencies in your community to start those meetings, at your facility and theirs, that will lead to working together in critical partnerships. They realize homeless people use your library. But what can you do together to minimize the impact and help a population that will never go away; only the faces and the names change.

In your town, such agencies might include the Salvation Army; St. Vincent de Paul Ministries; Catholic, Lutheran, or Methodist charities; soup kitchens; food banks; community medical clinics; and other faith-based services and church groups that want to provide homeless outreach and support in their communities, including those groups that address immigrant populations who are also homeless. The goal is to see the response to managing difficult or disruptive homeless people in your library as a *we* problem, not a *you* problem, as in, "What are *we* going to do about it?"

Community Mental Health Services

Understanding the Mental Health Mess

To say we have a significantly underfunded response to people with serious mental health problems in this country is akin to saying the Titanic had a bit of a run-in with some ice. It's impossible even to get a true handle on the issue of undiagnosed, untreated, unmedicated, poorly medicated souls who go on and off their necessary psychotropic drugs, because of their illness or because they cannot afford them, or who self-medicate with alcohol, meth, marijuana, and/or opiates to ease their physical and psychic pains. Many leading medical professionals, including television's Dr. Drew Pinsky, whose opinions I respect, say that we need to treat mental illness like a broken bone or cancer, something that is not the fault of the person who has it. The stigma of mental illness seems to have no end, as many long-suffering families of children or siblings with harrowing symptoms who have told sad stories to countless cops, social workers, physicians, psychologists, and psychiatrists can attest. Jails and prisons are usually the wrong place for people who are not murderously violent, but there are simply not enough treatment hospitals or available beds in existing mental health hospitals to help get those who need urgent care off the streets and into treatment.

The good news is that the county where your library sits has either an emergency room (ER) with access to behavioral health treatment specialists or a mental health hospital to help treat those people who are either troubled or troubling, or both. The bad news is, if you work in a large county, your county mental health (CMH) hospital is likely to be crowded, chaotic, and staffed with clinicians and others who are trying to do their best to help a daily and nightly wave of patients who self-admit, are brought in by their loved ones, or are hauled in by the police. It's more bad news if you work in a small county, where the CMH hospital may not be a dedicated mental health facility, but simply a bed or two in the local ER. In my Perfect Library World, we'd have enough CMH hospitals to cover the geographic and population numbers. Big cities and counties mean not enough beds. Small cities and counties mean not enough beds. The cycle continues.

Police work is often accurately described as "armed social work." Cops spend most of their time keeping the peace, not fighting crime. They are asked to make difficult decisions as to whether the person they have contacted is a danger to himself/herself, a danger to others, or gravely disabled. (Lying in the middle of traffic lanes on a busy street would be a good example of the latter.) Cops being cops and not trained in the intricacies of the *Diagnostic and Statistical Manual of Mental Disorders*, Fifth Edition (*DSM-V*), they will come to your library when you call them to deal with a potentially mentally ill patron. They will make a fairly quick value judgment as to whether the person in question falls into any of the three categories, and, if so, they will take this person, using their legal right to detain him or her, for an evaluation at the CMH hospital or its equivalent at the local ER. If the person being asked by the police agrees to go to the CMH hospital for treatment, then he or she goes in handcuffs in the back of the patrol car. If the person does not want to go for an evaluation, then you may witness a Gentle Smothering of Blue Bodies on top of the person until he or she stops wiggling around—same handcuffs, same ride in the back of the patrol car for the trip to the CMH hospital. (I was once slashed by a razor in the subject's hand during one of these stressful encounters. Another time, I fell on my partner and broke his pinky.) In other words, once the police arrive and make the decision to take the person in for an evaluation, it's no longer up for debate, discussion, or negotiation. And yet three additional problems arise in all this.

First, it is possible, and often likely, that after the police arrive, and using their best amateur psychology skills (unless they are riding with a PERT clinician or a psychiatric nurse, as happens in cities with the money for these specialized responders), they may decide the person is not a danger to self or others or gravely disabled, escort him out of the library with a stern warning not to return for the day, and leave. As an example, in California, the Welfare and Institutions Code defining danger to self, danger to others, and gravely disabled is 5150 W&I, and it's possible the cops on scene at your library will determine that your fellow is only 5149½ and he's not going anywhere with them.

Second, it is possible that the local CMH hospital is full, meaning it can no longer accept patients for some span of time. The police may agree with you and each other that the patron in question needs to go to the CMH hospital for his or her behaviors, but they simply cannot take the person because there is no room at the inn. This is usually a temporary condition, solved in a tedious way when another hospital, usually many miles or light-years away, agrees to serve as the backup site for the usual CMH hospital. You can guess how excited the police are to have to take someone from one end of the known galaxy to the other, and in truth, jurisdictional issues (aka funding and overtime concerns) or their own agency policies may not allow them to make a trek of any unusual distance with a mentally ill detainee.

Third, say the police have arrived and they agree with your initial phone call that the patron in question has displayed one or more of the behavioral indicators that warrant a trip to the CMH hospital. They escort said patron out the door, and in anywhere from sixty minutes to six hours, the patron is back at your library, furious at you for calling the cops on him or her. Welcome to a nightmare. What happened? Two possible things occurred:

- The cops took the patron to the CMH hospital and the doctors determined he was problematic, but not so problematic that they needed to keep him or her for any length of time. These poor souls are often given a shot of some medication or a few pills to tide them over until they can make an appointment, tomorrow or next week, to see a physician, a case worker, or the on-duty psychologist or psychiatrist.

■ The police take said patron to the CMH hospital, only to be told that the joint is swamped. There is no room for him or her, the person isn't unstable enough to warrant letting another more disturbed patient leave, so out the cops go, with instructions (and this is usually their agency policy) to take the person back to the exact spot where they first contacted them—in this case, your library. As a CMH hospital clinician once told me on a scary summer night when the moon was full, "Look, we have a one-hundred-bed psych hospital. If we have one hundred truly mentally ill patients and you cops bring in Patient one hundred one, we have to decide whether or not the new one comes in, which means we have to either release one of the one hundred or turn yours away. If yours is worse than the ones we already have, he or she gets in. If not, back he or she goes to the home planet of origin."

(Once the cops are told the detainee/patient won't be staying for treatment, sometimes they will leave him or her in the lobby of the CMH hospital and hightail it out of there. This is usually directly against their agency policy and can be perceived by many as inhumane. Their reasoning for this, of course, is that if they bring the person back to the library, he or she will act up again and this will require another response to the library, ending with perhaps a trip to jail this time. If they leave the person at the CMH hospital, which is often miles from the library, it's less likely that he or she will be able to make the trek, on foot, by bus, or light rail, back to the library to start trouble again. Interpret this as you will.)

The point to these three points? You have just witnessed the revolving door that is our current response to this nation's citizens with acute and chronic mental health problems. In my Perfect Library World, the patron is back at his or her usual table (hopefully with some helpful medication in his or her bloodstream), and there you go. It's not illegal to be mentally ill in this country, until you show that you want to hurt yourself or others or cannot care for your own safety.

Getting Help with the Mental Health Mess

Is this issue as bleak as I have described it? Yes. Is all hope lost for keeping seriously mentally ill patrons from creating havoc in your library? No. Let's go back to the value of the team approach.

Just as every county has to offer some form of a well-functioning or barely hanging-on hospital ER or mental health agency or facility, every county should also provide access to behavioral health services through one or more agencies. These folks are your primary stakeholders in the battle against the disruptive mentally ill patron, who may also have a substance abuse or homelessness issue to boot. The caring professionals (who face a lot of burnout and self-doubt in their jobs) in these departments can bring a lot of their resources to bear when it comes to helping you with your problematic patrons, but to reap these benefits, you have to establish those all-important relationships.

The behavioral health services agency is usually tasked with providing outpatient mental health services for children, adults, and seniors; substance abuse counseling; support from social workers; and referral to or treatment by psychologists or psychiatrists, and the agency also often runs the CMH hospital, day-use clinics, drug and alcohol abuse twelve-step meetings, and family mental health services to help parents and family members cope with the difficulties of a severely mentally ill child, adult, or sibling. Staff members work with a challenging client population, for not much money and little recognition by the public.

Your conversations and meetings with them can help with advice about how to help you and your colleagues deal with the mentally ill, plus provide some informational resources for your staff. Calling the police to take mentally ill patrons away or, if you have one, having your security guard escort them out is a solution, but not a satisfying one. Working with your county's mental health professionals on specific people (who they often know a lot about as well) means they can provide outreach, advice, on-scene interventions, advocacy, immediate resources for the mentally ill, and support. All of this may help you and them craft workable, longer-term solutions for a problem that is not easily solved or likely to go away.

Child Abuse Responders

I use this scenario in my workshops: You are a children's librarian and you are running a summer program for kids. Parents sign their kids in with you at the beginning of the day and sign them out with you at the end of the day. A woman shows up to get her child and it's clear that while you've been working, she has been drinking, a lot and all day. She signs her kid out on the clipboard, staggers off to the parking lot, loads her child into the car, and prepares to drive away. What do you do?

These are some answers I typically get: "I'd try to stop her from leaving." "I'd take her car keys." "I'd block her in the parking lot so she couldn't back out." "I'd tell her to come back inside while we talk about her being drunk in front of her kid." "I'd coax her back inside and have someone call the police." All of these answers are admirable, well-meaning, and wrong. The correct answer is this: "I'd follow her out to the parking lot, write down the license plate number and the make, model, and color of her car, and then I'd go back into the library and call 911 to notify the police. I would tell the dispatcher all of the information about the situation, her car, her last direction of travel, and her name and her child's name." In other words, you would be a good, professional witness.

Wanting to stop this woman from endangering her child is a reasonable response, for a cop, not for you. Cops are trained to do this and you aren't. You could get sued, injured, assaulted, or even killed trying to stop someone from driving away. In this situation, the dispatcher will relay the information to the police, who will run the plate and drive in the direction of the woman's house, looking for her along the way and hoping to catch her behind the wheel before or as she gets home. They will arrest her for drunk driving and give her child to a responsible family member while she goes to jail.

Let's change the scenario slightly: You're at the mall and you see an adult male whipping his son with a belt in front of everyone at the food court. What do you do? Again, I get a wide range of answers: "I'd stop him." "I'd start yelling." "I'd make a scene." "I'd try to get a mall security guard." Getting the mall security officer is a good choice, if you can find one. The officer might intervene and make a citizen's arrest (which I believe is necessary; a security officer shouldn't just "observe and report" when a child is being injured), or the mall officer will do what you can also do: Try to interrupt the process, ask the man to leave, follow him and the child to his car from a discreet distance, get the car's information, and, as with the drunk mom picking up her kid at your library, call the police to make a report. Part of the police response, if they can find the guy in time, is to make an arrest for felony child abuse, if possible, or at least get enough information to make a referral to Child Protective Services (CPS), which will then investigate and follow up as needed.

Most children's librarians are familiar with CPS, based on their role as mandated reporters for real or suspected child abuse. The report you make may not be the first one related to a particular parent or child. CPS has the same "frequent fliers" in its files as the mental health services people do. Reach out for CPS support in those situations that warrant a call.

Elder or Dependent Abuse Responders

As we continue with the "graying of America" (the median age in the country is about thirty-eight), we will see more opportunities for the abuse of elderly people or dependent adults (those over eighteen who have physical, emotional, or cognitive disabilities and require some form of care). Elder abuse or the abuse of dependent adults may come to your attention at the library when the family member or alleged caregiver either abandons the person he or she is supposed to take care of or physically or emotionally abuses the person in your presence. (I use the phrase *alleged caregiver* because the abusive ones often don't care, don't give much useful care, and are more like "takers" of the person's money or property.)

In San Diego County, we have nine Indian gaming casinos, one of the largest collections of gambling operations outside Nevada or New Jersey. It's not uncommon to see a crooked family member or alleged caregiver drop off a nice little old lady or gentleman at the library and then disappear for ten hours to play some blackjack at a casino, using that person's money. The irony is too painful.

More and more law enforcement agencies are either creating Elder Abuse Units or training their investigators to focus on elder abuse or dependent adult abuse crimes involving financial, physical, or emotional harm, neglect, or abandonment. This trend is a good sign, but until financial and physical elder abuse is a felony in all fifty states, which it isn't yet, these incidents will continue to surface occasionally at our libraries.

While you're not in the business of prying into people's personal lives, when it comes to your suspicions about elder abuse, you have the right to do something and the ability to do the right thing by reporting what you see to either the police or your county's APS agency. As with child abuse perpetrators, this may not be the first time the alleged caregiver's name has crossed the desk of APS.

Domestic Violence Responders

The emotional dynamics in relationships plagued with domestic violence are as cyclical as the participants. Their perspective gets skewed. When we help domestic violence victims because they want our help, we are "rescuing" them. When we try to help them when they don't want our help, we are "harassing" them. Despite the best efforts of cops, prosecutors, judges, social workers, divorce attorneys, family members, and victim advocacy groups, sometimes people in domestic violence relationships participate in bringing about their own deaths by not understanding the absolute potential for a fatal outcome if they don't get away safely and for good.

Domestic violence can cross the threshold into your library in many forms: Teenagers in a dating relationship; same-sex relationships; and even relationships between similarly aged elderly people. The issue crosses all gender, racial, age, and socioeconomic boundaries. I have seen female library staffers have the courage (with a capital C) to talk to a woman in a domestic violence relationship when she comes into the library alone and away from her batterer. They gave her informational resources related to counseling, shelters, and a twenty-four-hour hotline. Is this crossing a boundary that goes beyond the job description of a library employee's usual duties, or is this being a good citizen and a compassionate human being toward a person in crisis? I vote for the latter, with a caveat: It's easy for library employees to become overly involved in a situation related to an elderly patron, a child who is abandoned in the library, or a domestic violence victim. If you're a supervisor, commend your employees for their care and concern, but remind them that they need to be careful not to lose their perspective and get too caught up in a situation that has legal ramifications, safety concerns, and the potential for bringing violence into the library. It's best to call the police and/or a victim advocacy group and let the professionals intervene.

If you politely but persistently ask these various stakeholders—homeless services providers, mental health professionals, domestic violence victim advocacy groups, and child abuse and elder abuse prevention specialists— to come to a meeting at your facility, you can then move forward with a discussion about the problem patron issues your library faces and maybe even be able to show those visitors the exact people you are dealing with. You can't get help if you don't initiate the contact. Make those necessary and important first phone calls, make the follow-up calls, set the meetings and attend them religiously, and keep moving the process forward. Don't take a first no as a final answer.

CHAPTER 9

Staff Development for a Safer Library

Results, Not Just Rules

T oo many rules doth not a safe library make (said Shakespeare or Yoda, I think). The functions of your policies and procedures and codes of conduct are to define boundaries for patrons, help your staff enforce what needs to be enforced, and create a workable, reasonable, and appropriate environment for people to use and enjoy your library.

The entire employee manual for the Seattle, Washington–based Nordstrom department store chain is a five-by-eight-inch gray card with these sixty-seven words:

> Our number one goal is to provide outstanding customer service. Set both your personal and professional goals high. We have great confidence in your ability to achieve them, so our employee handbook is very simple. We have only one rule. Our One Rule: Use good judgment in all situations. Please feel free to ask your department manager, store manager, or Human Resources any questions at any time.

Nordstrom was founded in 1901. For any company, especially in the retail rag trade, to last over 100 years is impressive. The existence of their One Rule gets debated online by business, HR, and legal people who don't believe you can run a retail chain with over 200 stores using an index card as your guiding principle. (President Lincoln used 272 words in the Gettysburg Address, long considered one of the most moving and concise political speeches given in America.) Does Nordstrom have an inches-thick policy and procedures manual that covers all of the usual employee HR issues from schizophrenia to dandruff? Of course. The legal requirements for Nordstrom are the same as for any other company, so the company has plenty of written rules about breaks and lunches, time cards, employee discounts, progressive discipline, termination, harassment prevention, the promotion process, health care benefits, dress code, and so on. Such formalities are just not their preferred way of communicating with their employees, who are valued deeply. (There is much employee empowerment in those sixty-seven words, an approach other businesses might adopt. Most content in the pages of a typical HR manual is often driven by an organization's attorneys, who are trying to account for every possible misunderstanding that could lead to litigation.)

Does this mean you can run an entire library operation using an index card? Yes, if you operate it out of your house and you're the only employee and the only patron. But does it make sense to create plain-English, common-sense rules for your employees and your patrons? If possible, yes—just as we discussed in Chapter 2 on the value of clear codes of conduct.

Training to the Rescue!

Perhaps. How do we prove our training programs are working? If employees go through so-called hard-skills (e.g., using software, equipment, or machinery) training classes, it's usually easy to verify that what they were taught worked. With soft-skills training—behavior-based, knowledge-based, experiential, or compliance programs—it's tougher. How do you prove your sexual harassment awareness and prevention program worked? One possible measure is the absence of the problem—no complaints, no investigations. But does that mean the problem is not an issue or that some employees are still fearful about reporting it no matter how many times we tell them of their obligations?

Since I teach safety and security workshops and workplace violence prevention sessions, I take no small amount of pride in the fact that, so far, no one from my client organizations has been injured or killed in the weeks, months, and years following my sessions. I also measure my success with these tough training topics in several ways: I take the group through a pretest and a posttest; I give quick oral quizzes throughout; I use a lot of open-ended, Socratic questions to elicit their answers; I remind them of the concepts and new vocabulary frequently; and at the beginning of the workshop I often give them a cheat sheet, which is a summary of the slides, that I also review at the end. I ask the management who brought me in to remind the employees about the concepts during staff meetings, using all-hands e-mails, and in one-on-one coaching sessions.

The return on your training investment dollar is both critical and hard to measure. Both the trainer and the organization share the responsibility to see that training sticks, the concepts are applied, and the participants show changes in their behavior or performance.

Training Naysayers

During my library security workshops, it's not uncommon to see a participant sitting in the room with a look on his or her face that I can read from twenty-five feet away: "All this communication and customer service stuff sounds good here in the classroom, but what he's talking about doesn't work in the 'real world.' He doesn't know what we're facing here every day." (Yes, I do.) I'm not (usually) offended by this perspective—I hear it from a lot of police officers I train too—so I address it as soon as I see evidence of it, if not before: "There are no absolutes when it comes to dealing with people. These techniques may work the first time you try them or the fifth time. You may need to try them in different ways, with different people. You may get some people to cooperate some of the time, and some people will not cooperate, no matter what you say or do. You know people want to vent, to be heard, to be validated, and to protect their self-esteem. Do the best you can, change the ratios of confrontation, use the concept of 'alignment,' get help from a boss or a coworker, and if the situation turns threatening, call the police. I can't promise you success always, but I believe these approaches will work if you use them consistently. I know for certain that they won't work if you never try them."

Let's review why people go to training workshops in the first place. One reason is that they are ordered to go by their bosses or their organization. (I always ask, "Is this training voluntary or mandatory?" When I hear the group shout, "Mandatory!" I say, "Many thanks for volunteering to go to this mandatory training.") Another reason to go to training is to get out of work, off the library floor, or out of your back office, for the morning or the afternoon. This is not a bad thing. The change of scenery will do you good. Sometimes it's fun to go to training to see some old friends or catch up with colleagues you haven't seen for a bit. I've always found library people to be quite social with one another, even if they are a lot of introverts trapped in an extrovert's job (which is how I describe myself). There is always a lot of chatter at the beginning of my sessions and during the breaks, while the participants share their stories about nightmare patrons who came to mind during the discussions.

The primary reason to go to training, of course, is to learn something new, but not just that; it's also about being able to apply what you learned after you leave. Sitting for hours in a room and not taking a single note, not jotting down a single thought, not reviewing the handouts even once, and not giving much effort to the discussions or the exercises won't hurt the instructor's feelings, but such lack of effort will hurt the person who fails to take advantage of the training as well as his or her organization, which is paying the employee to be there. So why not pitch in and participate?

There's another great reason to go to training: You can verify that what you're currently doing is correct. Since I consider myself chronically over-trained, I find myself in this position frequently. I still go to a lot of training classes, attend a lot of conferences, and log on to a lot of webinars, and I completely review the presenters' materials even if I already know the subject well. (Einstein once said, "The only thing that interferes with my learning is my education.") I'm always looking to pick up a story, an example, a tool, or a solution that makes the session worthwhile for me. Not everything a presenter says will be useful for me, but if he or she gives me one or two great ideas per hour, I'm satisfied. You should attend trainings of all kinds and do likewise. Through training, your organization shows that it considers you to be an important asset, worthy of exposure to new approaches to help you do your job safely and successfully. Take what you're given in the training environment and run with it. It's yours to keep.

Some Final Thoughts

- Ask all supervisors and employees to be firm, fair, consistent, and assertive in the application of library codes of conduct and safety and security policies.
- Put the code of conduct on large posters that are visible near the entrances and other common areas.

- Be courageous and use civil stay-away and permanent or temporary restraining orders for chronically problematic people.
- Establish a relationship with the police officer or sheriff's deputy who has responsibility for your facility.
- Create and nurture relationships with the subject matter experts in your regional area, from both public- and private-sector organizations, who deal with specific types of problem patrons as part of their work.
- Remember that asking for help from coworkers or your boss when dealing with difficult patrons does not mean you don't know how to do your job. Sometimes changing the ratios of confrontation can make a big difference. There is safety in numbers (your coworker can not only watch you handle the situation, but can also be a witness to whatever happens).
- Report security issues and problem patrons to library directors or supervisors, who should in turn reward the staff members who do so.
- Remember that it's the results, not just the rules. Think on your feet at the same time as you follow your facility's policies. Be willing to do whatever it takes to solve the patron's problem, safely and effectively, so you and your colleagues can be safe and effective.

Top Ten Security Tips

With homage to the career of David Letterman, here are ten ideas to help you succeed:

1. **Trust your intuition.** Listen to that little voice and act on it.

2. **Be assertively polite.** And be firm and fair and consistent.

3. **Try a lighter touch first.** A little humor can change the dynamics of any potentially difficult conversation with a patron because it proves you're a human being too.

4. **Know when to change the ratios of confrontation.** Be ready to bring in more help, from a colleague, your boss, or the police.

5. **Stay in Condition Yellow when dealing with the public.** Condition Red says get out of there or protect yourself. Move into Condition White only when you are safe in the back or on your break, when you can then relax and recharge. Pay attention to your safety the rest of the time.

6. **Change your position; use space, distance, and other proxemic barriers.** Stay out of the face-to-face zone. Approach all angry or disturbed patrons at a slight angle and stay at least an arm's length away (plus a bit more). Use desks, counters, chairs, shelves, windows, locked doors, or the telephone as a barrier if the situation calls for it.

7. **Practice "If…, then…" thinking.** Strive to be so good at this that no comment, behavior, or action by a patron catches you off guard. Anticipate that a patron might be erratic, eccentric, or unusual, and have your verbal or physical response ready.

8. **Report every incident during which you or others felt afraid.** What gets measured gets managed. The frequent use of Security Incident Reports can help the library leadership team keep track of ongoing security issues and address them, using data and not word-of-mouth stories.

9. **Work as a team.** Use the power of your colleagues and their intuition and experience to help you. Get assistance from outside the library, using community or government resources to help you solve long-standing problems involving the mentally ill, homeless, teenagers, and other patrons who impact the business of the library.

10. **Be a Shepherd.** Take care of yourself first, your colleagues second, and the patrons third, in that order.

Going Forward with Safety and Security

Perhaps safe libraries should start with a complete and radical redesign of the actual use concept. Maybe we need to turn some branches into "books and periodicals only" locations, with no Internet access and better enforcement of the codes of conduct. Maybe we could convert some branches into Internet cafés, with no books, but lots of screens to sit at and a tech-trained staff to help (and also better enforcement of the codes of conduct). Maybe some branches could be converted to children-only libraries, where unaccompanied kids have to be signed in and out by a parent, lone adult males are not allowed inside, and the Internet content is filtered. Last, what about instituting a total commitment to safety in the library that mandates trained security officers, a better police response, rock-solid enforcement of codes of conduct, and support from city and county leaders and elected officials to make sure staff members and normal patrons have a safe place to work and visit?

We know Jared Lee Loughner as the man who showed up at a community event in Tucson, Arizona, on January 8, 2011, and shot and wounded US Representative Gabrielle Giffords. He shot and killed six people and wounded thirteen more. In the months and even years before the shootings, as described by his friends, he acted highly paranoid, anxious, and suspicious, full of rants against the government and disconnected from reality—in short, a garden-variety schizophrenic with violent tendencies. (I paid a lot of money for my psychology degree; I might as well use it.)

Loughner had been expelled from Pima Community College because he scared fellow classmates with his erratic behaviors and ranting about the injustices he perceived, his constant confrontations with teachers, and his postings on YouTube of several odd and rambling videos that he had taped on campus. The Pima Community College police sent four officers to Loughner's home who told him he could not return to campus until he was cleared by a mental health clinician. (The CBS show *60 Minutes* and Scott Pelley did an excellent segment on Loughner called "Descent Into Madness," available online at www.cbsnews.com/videos/tucson-descent-into-madness.) A good predictor of future erratic, deviant, threatening, predatory, or violent behavior is past erratic, deviant, threatening, predatory, or violent behavior. Loughner had previously been kicked out of the Tucson Public Library for disruptive behavior there as well. The moral of this sad story: You never know who will come through your door. We can't pick our patrons; we have what could be called a "trapped customer relationship," meaning we get who we get. You can manage your responses to patrons' behaviors, thank them for their cooperation, and invite them back, within reason, of course.

In our world, there are sheep, shepherds, and wolves. Too many people are sheep, too few people are shepherds, and there are a lot of wolves out there. There are not enough cops or sheriff's deputies to protect us all. You need to be a Shepherd. This concept has nothing to do with the Bible or religion. It has to do with taking care of people. I've been a Shepherd my entire adult life, starting when I became a cop at twenty-one. I think about caring for the safety of others every single day, and so should you. Take care of yourself first because you can't help others if you're not safe. Take care of your coworkers next, and expect them to do the same for you. Then take care of the patrons, especially the ones who are the most vulnerable. You don't have to be heroic, just courageous. You don't have to risk your life, just show your courage. Feel your fears and overcome them with slow, steady, and deep stress management breathing. Pay attention and be a good witness for the police if you see a crime. Stay in Condition Yellow, which is safe and aware and alert, whenever you're on the library floor, at the desk, or in contact with any patron. What happened yesterday is no predictor of today. You owe it to yourself, your family, your colleagues, your organization, and your patrons to use your skills, intuition, and common sense to do the right thing when it comes to security. Be a Shepherd.

Library Security Survey Checklist

Perimeter Security Review

- Walk the exterior of the building, including the parking lots. What is your overall impression?
- Are there graffiti and trash, homeless people, or potentially problematic businesses (liquor stores, homeless shelters, teen centers, halfway houses, bus stations) nearby? Landscaping needs? Hazards?
- What are the area crime rates? Neighborhood "spillover" issues? Check your county's or state's online Megan's Law database for registered sex offenders in your ZIP code.
- Are there exterior building lights? Parking lot lights? Lighting for stairwells and elevators? (This illustrates the need for a night visit to the facility as well.)
- Do doors close and lock tightly? Any hardware, lock, hinge, or gate problems?
- Are utility panels and shutoffs secured?
- Are there barriers, proper signage, fencing, and bollards in front of the doors to prevent cars from coming too close?

Facility Security Review

- Are access control devices in place?
- Does the building have multiple tenants? Is it a shared-use facility? Is there a landlord?
- What are the exterior door controls—key card readers, mechanical keypads, or hard keys?

- Is the lobby unsecured or secured? Staffed or empty?
- Do employees come and go through the same doors as visitors? Are there exterior or interior cameras?
- Does the building have loading docks? Warehouse doors? Roof access?
- Are burglar or panic alarms in place? Fire suppression? Knox-Boxes with keys for the fire department inside?
- Are all locations that could attract a child secured? (This includes break rooms or kitchens, cleaning supply closets, utility closets, adult restrooms, and basement doors.)

HR, Security, Emergency, Evacuation Policy and Procedure Review

- Review all HR policies related to termination procedures, keys or key card and badge collections, and network log-offs.
- Review all security policies related to access control, vendor escorts, alarm codes, and employees working after hours.
- Review all emergency and evacuation floor plans or maps, policies, and floor warden systems for fire, bomb threat, earthquake, weather, and active shooter lockdown evacuations.

Information Security Review

- Meet with your city or county IT representatives about access control for server rooms, utility closets, mailrooms, and copy rooms and the use of asset tags for laptops, computers, projectors, televisions, flat screens, tablets, or other theft-sensitive electronic items.
- Discuss off-site backup procedures, emergency power, prevention of network intrusion, hacking, and related cyber threats.
- Review fire control rooms, equipment, and procedures.
- Discuss updated PA system announcements through the phone system.
- Review employee and patron information hard-copy file protections.

Vendor Management Procedures

- Review or create a "Red Book" for circulation desk employees that contains all emergency numbers, call trees, building plans, and evacuation procedures.
- Review all vendor access and escort procedures.
- Discuss trespass policies.
- Review where vendors work or wait.
- Verify vendor key control and access: Janitorial services, landscaping, package deliveries, soda or water, copier repair, and building maintenance.
- Discuss patron access control issues and improvements to keep them out of employees-only areas.

Internal/External Theft Controls

- What are the most theft-sensitive items in the facility? Computers, projectors, laptops, and tablets? Recyclable metals? Printers, toner, and office supplies? Software? Postage? Warehouse equipment?
- Review all inventory control and flow procedures, from delivery to shipping. Are certain items caged or stored under lock and key?
- Discuss all past internal or external theft incidents.

Facility First-Aid Procedures

- Review the locations of all first-aid kits, AED devices, and needles/sharps boxes.
- Review all first-aid training materials for AEDs, CPR, and minor injury responses.
- Remind all employees whether they need to dial just 911 or 9-911.

Fiduciary Instrument Controls

- Review the locations of all drop boxes, cash drawers, registers, safes, and vaults.
- Review all policies related to cash, check, and fiduciary instrument handling; blank checks; credit card machines; bank

deposit procedures; petty cash disbursement; and the use of armored car services.

- Discuss internal audit procedures.

Security Guards

- Are they in-house or proprietary? Do they have powers of arrest?
- Review all posted orders for each guard position.
- Meet with the guard contractor to update contracts and to create or modify orders and duties.
- Do guards serve a reception function? Are they responsible for panic alarm, burglar alarm, and/or open-door responses?
- How do guards respond to a violent patron?
- Review guard equipment lists: Facility keys, call tree lists, radios, and time clocks. Make sure guards have working flashlights for power emergencies.

Law Enforcement and Fire Department Interactions

- Verify the dispatch numbers for all local law enforcement (police and sheriff), and fire department, and Emergency Medical Services (EMS) responders. Ask employees to put those numbers in their cell phones.
- Make sure building addresses are large and visible.
- Identify key law enforcement and fire personnel commanders for future support with drills, active shooter responses, or follow-up after police, fire, or EMS responses to the facility.

Workplace Violence Response

- Review all workplace violence prevention policies: Temporary restraining orders, domestic violence at work, and new weapons possession laws for patrons with concealed weapons permits.
- Review all workplace violence training materials for employee orientations or in-service programs.
- Verify Employee Assistance Program (EAP) contact information.
- Discuss the formation of a Threat Assessment Team (TAT).

- Discuss active shooter training, using the model based on the *Run. Hide. Fight.* video (Department of Homeland Security/ City of Houston, Texas).
- Identify potential safe room/shelter-in-place locations and make changes to door hardware and windows to ensure these areas are secure in a lockdown/shelter-in-place situation.

Emergency and Security Drills

- Discuss the need for emergency, evacuation, and security-related drills with senior management. Schedule fire, weather, earthquake, or active shooter drills at least once per year.
- Meet with community first responders to discuss these drills.
- Train all employees before all drills and debrief all employees after the drills.
- Create specific PA announcements, including one for an active shooter situation (e.g., "There is an unusual incident in area X").

Site Security Survey Reports

- Date, time, and location of site assessment and participants.
- Executive summary of key points, with photos.
- Exterior and interior site findings.
- Security improvement suggestions (vendor neutral).
- Appendixes: Emergency, evacuation, and active shooter procedures; policy improvements; employee training; risks; legal issues; targets; and threats.
- Drafts, confidentiality, limited circulation, and fact checks.

Implementing the Results

- Hold stakeholder meetings with department heads.
- Distribute report copies on a need-to-have basis.
- Address any employee concerns or union issues.
- Submit the report for review by the employee safety committee and legal department.
- Hold training classes, work on policy development and approval, and consider equipment purchases and installations, capital improvements, and physical facility changes.

Effective Follow-Up

- Don't write a report that dies on the shelf.
- Keep the stakeholder team on task and on time.
- Set hard deadlines for department head reviews.
- Set thirty-day, ninety-day, six-month, and one-year follow-ups.
- Balance the need for changes with new incidents.
- Remember the Big Three: Cost, Culture, and Feasibility.

Sample Library Security Suggestions for Site Survey Reports

- Review the posted orders for the contract guard company and meet with the company's site manager to make location-specific changes or service improvements.
- For library locations that have lockers for their employees' use, discuss creating a locker policy: All full- and part-time staff have no expectation of privacy when using library-supplied lockers. Employees are prohibited from bringing or storing firearms, weapons, ammunition, fireworks, illegal drugs, alcohol, or any contraband. All library-provided lockers are subject to search based on reasonable suspicion for any of the aforementioned items.
- Discuss the current or draft policies about Internet/Wi-Fi use for patrons using their own devices (iPads, tablets, etc.).
- For children's rooms, discuss how to create signage that discourages adults without kids (or who are not looking at books for their kids) from hanging out there; for example: "This area is for reserved for our young readers and their parents or relatives only." Staff can often tell which adults have a reason for being in the children's area and which ones are either predatory or looking for the wrong place to sit. The presence of these people can be intimidating to kids and parents.
- Review the background screening process for the literacy program volunteers.

- Encourage staff to report problematic patrons, either to their supervisors, as part of regular staff meeting discussions about safety and security, or to the police or sheriff's department.
- Create a circulation desk employee "Red Book" that contains emergency contact numbers, evacuation plans, building maps, utility shutoff information, employee rosters, and other important data that staffers (full- or part-time) can refer to in an emergency.
- Continue to train staff about employee and patron evacuation and/or lockdown policies and procedures. Each facility should have posted evacuation instructions and staff training on how and when to notify the police, sheriff, or fire department and on how to protect themselves and patrons during potential or actual fires, earthquakes, natural and equipment-failure disasters, and active shooter responses. These emergency-related policies should include the establishment or updating of phone trees, emergency callback numbers and procedures, and staff notifications.
- Monitor the theft rate for materials and continue to discuss the need for vigilance and staff response at the circulation desk to deter thefts.
- Ask staff to monitor and enforce the existing policies on patrons bringing actual service animals (specifically trained dogs) into the facility versus comfort animals (cats, rats, birds, snakes, etc.). This is a safety and hygiene issue faced by many libraries throughout the United States.
- Remind all staff that they may need to dial 9-911 to reach emergency help, not just 911. Ask them to put the dispatch number for the police or sheriff's department into their cell phones.

Sample Staff Training Exercises

These exercises are useful for staff meetings when the discussion turns to security-related or patron-behavior issues. If you're running the meeting, these three exercises can give you a good sense of the current state of employee perceptions about their contacts with challenging patrons. You may want to print them out and have someone capture the answers, comments, and ideas on an easel pad or whiteboard, for further discussion.

Exercise #1: Name That Patron!

Instructions: Working with your team, write the letter of the patron next to the sentence that seems to fit best. There could be more than one answer for several of the statements.

a. Internet desk hog
b. Teenager and friends
c. Sleeping transient
d. Thief
e. Screaming patron
f. Vandal/tagger

g. Violent patron with a weapon
h. Porn site enthusiast
i. Internet time waster
j. Disgruntled/entitled patron

1. ____ "Are you feeling okay? Are you sick or anything?"
2. ____ "There's about ten minutes left on your time, and other folks are waiting. I just wanted you to know in case you have to print out something."

3. ____ "If you don't stop yelling, I won't be able to understand you. If I can't understand you, I won't be able to help."

4. ____ "You'll be on the computer from 3:00 p.m. to 4:00 p.m. The screen locks up after that."

5. ____ "Wow! You seem really upset! What can I do to help?"

6. ____ "You seem to be really interested in that DVD. Can I help you find something in particular?"

7. ____ "Thanks for helping me out. I know I can count on you to show your friends how it's done."

8. ____ "I'll be watching from right over there if you need me."

9. ____ "Will the guy who printed the naked pictures please come pick them up?"

10. ____ "My name is Mary. I know you don't want to hurt anyone. What's your name?"

(Some smarty-pantses in my workshops have suggested to me, not untruthfully, that answer *h*, porn site enthusiast, could be a reasonable response for most of these. That wasn't my intention, but I don't disagree either.)

ANSWER KEY: 1. c; 2. a or i; 3. e or j; 4. a or i; 5. e or j; 6. d; 7. b; 8. d or f; 9. h; 10. g

Exercise #2: Patron Role-Plays

Instructions: Break your staff into small groups of at least three. Using the following familiar scenarios, have each staffer play the part of the Patron, the Library Employee, and the Observer. Ask the Observer to hold his or her comments until the end and give the two role-players some useful feedback. Provide best-practices answers to the role-players and allow them enough time to debrief with each other and the whole group.

1. A patron is using the Internet and soon goes over his one-hour time limit. Other patrons are lining up at your desk to use the Internet too. One patron says to you, "Hey! I'm next and he's hogging the computer. I need to get online now! Either you do something about him or I will!"

2. An adult comes to your desk and it's clear she's very angry. She's accompanied by her thirteen-year-old son. She says, "Yesterday, one of you people told my boy he had to leave because

he was making too much noise. I want somebody to tell me why he was told this, and I want to speak to the one who made him go!" (Yesterday was your day off and the employee in question is off today.)

3. An elderly gentleman is at the circulation desk trying to check out two videos. His borrowing privileges have been revoked due to overdue notices, substantial fines, and missing items that were never returned. He says to you, "You're just picking on me because I'm old! I know my rights! You have to let me have this stuff!"

4. During a summertime field trip sponsored by the local day camp, you see several children riding on the book carts, jumping on the tables, and pounding the computer keyboards. You approach the camp counselor, who tells you, in a defensive way, "What's the big deal? They're just kids letting off a little steam. Weren't you young once?"

5. Two teenage couples are in the library near closing time. It's clear from their physical behavior that each is highly interested in his or her date. Both couples are making out quite visibly and other patrons are embarrassed. One of the boys stops his activity and says to you, "What are you looking at?" The other boy joins in and taunts you with the same question. Now what do you do?

6. An older woman approaches you at the reference desk to complain about noise being made by a couple of young children laughing and playing. She says, "Libraries are supposed to be quiet places. What's wrong with parents these days? Those kids should be using the children's area. What are you going to do about this?" You've been busy with another patron and haven't registered any more noise coming from the children than from the adult users.

7. A man in his thirties who frequents the library almost daily was seen with a young boy, who looked about twelve, playing video games on the man's laptop computer. The man and the boy had both been seen in the library before but never together, so the staff grew suspicious that the young boy might be influenced by the adult into viewing inappropriate websites or playing

inappropriate videos or other games. You approach the man and he says, "Go away! My new friend and I are doing fine without your help."

8. On Fridays the library closes at 8:00 p.m. As you leave for the night, you see a thirteen-year-old girl sitting on a bench in front of the building. You ask her if someone is coming for her; she tells you her mom was supposed to pick her up at 7:00 but she is not answering her cell phone. She appears old enough to take care of herself but looks uneasy. It's already 8:20 p.m. What do you do?

9. A fifty-year-old man who is developmentally disabled spends all his time on the Internet. He needs to be reminded of the Internet usage rules and not to make fun of other people or to stare at young women in the library. He gets dropped off by a caregiver, who rarely stays very long with him once he's inside. The female staff members feel uncomfortable around him, although he has not done anything physically toward them. What do you do?

10. A burly guy comes into the library and seems very intimidating. He always wants to use the exact same Internet computer each time, and he gets visibly upset when another patron is using "his computer." He has confronted people who get too close to him or ask when he will be done using the computer. Staffers are afraid to speak with him because he seems paranoid and suspicious. Any suggestions?

11. A first-grader comes in every Saturday morning with her grandmother for children's reading hour. The child seems happy playing with other kids but actually seems fearful of her grandmother. When staff members try to engage with the grandmother, she acts like she doesn't speak English, although some have heard her talking to the child in English. When it's time to leave, the child cries and doesn't want to go. The grandmother gets angry and pulls her roughly out the door. What should you do?

12. A middle-aged man likes to dominate all conversations in the library. His voice is loud and other staff and patrons seem rattled or offended by his mannerisms. He comes into the

library about once per week but doesn't seem to remember how to use the Internet, so he makes a lot of demands for staff time to explain the simplest things to him, over and over again. Staffers are not sure if this is real or if he is messing with them. Suggestions?

Exercise #3: Difficult Patrons and Getting Additional Support

Consider the types of potentially difficult patrons who frequent your facility. Think about their behavior and how it may concern you, coworkers, or other patrons. Answer the following questions:

- Who are the three most difficult patrons in your facility (either by name or by description)?
- What do they do that calls your attention to them?
- How do they hurt your business?
- What have you done to get them to comply that has worked?
- What have you done to get them to comply that has failed?

List the liaison partners available in your community to help with these most difficult patrons:

- Law enforcement contacts?
- Community agencies, support groups, or publicly or privately run social welfare groups?
- Where can we get "outside the box" assistance from certain experts or groups?

Want Less Stress? Try More BREADS

Library work is challenging, rewarding, and, let's face it, stressful. We all need realistic tools for stress management, not things that take superhuman effort or a huge lifestyle shift, but things that work. Therein lies the power of BREADS. Each of the following techniques will help you with the personal and professional stressors you face at every point during your career. If you can focus on these six techniques every day, you will see important differences in your energy level, enthusiasm for life, and the quality of your relationships as well as improvements in your work, patience, and mental and physical health.

Breathing: Stress-related breathing is short, shallow, and rapid. Stress-managed breathing is long, deep, and slow. All skilled athletes learn to control their breathing during their sport activities and especially just before they perform specific moves. You cannot function effectively if your breathing is out of control. Practice breathing slowly and deeply, concentrating on the length of each breath and spending a moment on those transitions between the end of each inhalation and the start of each exhalation.

Relaxation: This does not mean put your feet up with a cold drink and watch television. Using focused relaxation, self-hypnosis, or meditation for stress control means you should try to find a minimum of ten minutes each day, in a safe and quiet place, to close your eyes and simply do one thing: Breathe slowly, counting from 100 down to 1 (okay, so that's two things). If you can make this a part of your everyday routine, like brushing your teeth (and just as for good tartar control, twice a day would be even better), you will actually want to start extending the time.

Exercise: Running a marathon is not necessary to get beneficial, stress-relieving exercise. Just walk, daily, for about thirty minutes. Walking is easier on your joints, burns calories if you move along at a lively pace (about 130 steps per minute is a good clip), and is a great social activity for connecting with your spouse or partner, friends, colleagues, or dog. Exercise helps you get better sleep, burns your excess stress energy from the day, minimizes depression, and supports your heart and lungs.

Attitude: In two words, you can better manage your personal and professional stress when you are *relentlessly positive*. People who see the worst in everyone and in everything are no fun to be around. Not all of the world is bad. Those same people who always see their glasses (or their checking accounts) as half empty rather than half full bring down everyone around them. Leucadia, California–based psychologist and longtime stress expert Dr. Brian Alman says it best: "Successful people have one foot in the present and the other in the future. Miserable people have one foot in the present and the other stuck in the past." Find the good in the situation you're in. We live in the best country on the planet. Unlike a few billion other people around the world who have no money and bad water, we are blessed with flush toilets, constant electric power, and quality television.

Diet: Out with the bad carbs (diet and regular sodas, candy, bagels, white rice, pasta, fries, packaged flour, and sugar-loaded foods) and in with the lean proteins, more veggies, complex carbohydrates, fruits, nuts, more water, and vitamin supplements. Food is a drug, and it changes your mood for the good or the bad (common culprits include caffeine, liquor, sugar, and fats). Small changes, like cutting portion sizes, avoiding most fast foods, studiously drinking two glasses of water before each meal, avoiding carbs after dinner, or adding more fiber, make a big difference over time. Your body needs fuel, but it needs the right kind of fuel. What you eat makes a difference in how you think and feel and even in how you sleep.

Sleep: We are the products of a sleep-deprived culture. People who say they can get by on four to six hours a night are actually harming themselves. Lack of sleep affects your hormones (which can give you belly fat), judgment, concentration, and interactions with people. If you feel tired all the time, resolve to get more and better sleep than you do now. People sleep in ninety-minute cycles. If you can adjust when you go to bed so that you wake up at the end of a ninety-minute cycle, you'll feel better. Consider this: Have you ever gotten only four hours of sleep and woken up feeling fairly refreshed? Have you ever gotten ten hours of sleep and woken up feeling like a zombie? In the first scenario, you woke up at the end of a ninety-minute cycle, and in the second you woke up in the middle of one. So if you go to bed at 10:30 p.m. and get up at 6:00 a.m., you will usually feel better than if you go to bed at 10:00 p.m. and get up at 6:00 a.m. Keep your bedroom dark, quiet (use a white noise fan or earplugs), and cool while sleeping. Don't fight with your spouse or partner in the bedroom; go to another part of the house. Your bedroom should be a place of peace.

Try these six important steps as you go through your work and personal life. They are easy to do and practical and provide you with a memorable acronym for stress management and relaxation, which is something we can all use.

Resources

Albrecht, Karl. *Service America! Doing Business in the New Economy.* Burr Ridge, IL: Irwin, 1985.

Albrecht, Karl. *Social Intelligence: The New Science of Success.* San Francisco, CA: Wiley, 2005.

Albrecht, Steve. *Tough Training Topics: A Presenter's Survival Guide.* San Francisco, CA: Wiley, 2006.

ASIS (American Society for Industrial Security) International. www .asisonline.org.

Blair, J. Pete, and Katherine W. Schweit. *A Study of Active Shooter Incidents, 2000–2013.* Washington, DC: Texas State University and Federal Bureau of Investigation, US Department of Justice, 2014. www .fbi.gov/news/stories/2014/september/fbi-releases-study-on-ac-tive-shooter-incidents/pdfs/a-study-of-active-shooter-incidents-in-the-u.s.-between-2000-and-2013.

Calhoun, Frederick S., and Stephen W. Weston. *Contemporary Threat Management.* San Diego, CA: Specialized Training Services, 2003.

Calhoun, Frederick S., and Stephen W. Weston. *Threat Assessment and Management Strategies: Identifying the Howlers and Hunters.* Boca Raton, FL: CRC Press, 2009.

de Becker, Gavin. *The Gift of Fear: Survival Signals That Protect Us from Violence.* Boston, MA: Little, Brown, 1997.

Gilmartin, Kevin M. *Emotional Survival for Law Enforcement: A Guide for Officers and Their Families.* Tucson, AZ: E-S Press, 2002.

Gladwell, Malcolm. *Blink: The Power of Thinking without Thinking.* New York: Little, Brown, 2005.

Infopeople. Library training resources. www.infopeople.org.

Mantell, Michael, and Steve Albrecht. *Ticking Bombs: Defusing Violence in the Workplace.* Burr Ridge, IL: Irwin Professional Publishing, 1994.

O'Toole, Mary Ellen, and Alisa Bowman. *Dangerous Instincts: Use an FBI Profiler's Tactics to Avoid Unsafe Situations.* New York, NY: Plume, 2012.

Patterson, Kerry, Joseph Grenny, Ron McMillan, and Al Switzler. *Crucial Conversations: Tools for Talking When Stakes Are High.* New York, NY: McGraw-Hill, 2002.

SHRM (Society for Human Resource Management) Online. www.shrm .org.

Thompson, George J., and Jerry B. Jenkins. *Verbal Judo: The Gentle Art of Persuasion.* Updated ed. New York: William Morrow, 2013.

US Department of Homeland Security. www.dhs.gov.

US Secret Service, National Threat Assessment Center. "Research and Publications: Exceptional Case Study Project (ESCP)." www .secretservice.gov/ntac.shtml.

INDEX

A

access control, 93, 110
active listening, 88
Adult Protective Services (APS), 66, 130
aisles, blocking, 40
alarms, 111
Albrecht, Karl, 21, 23–26
alertness, degrees of, 15–16, 138
alignment, 18–19, 50
Alman, Brian, 156
anger management, 17–18
animals, 38–39, 57–58
asking questions, 88
assaults, 32–33. *See also* shooters; workplace violence
attitude, 156

B

behavior
    addressing problematic, 29–31
    documenting bad, 19
    most challenging, 31–41
    patterns in, 20, 139
behavioral health services, 127
bikes, 36
Blink: The Power of Thinking without Thinking (Gladwell), 92
blocking aisles, 40
boundaries, over the phone, 23
BREADS, 155–157
breathing, control of, 17–18, 155

C

Calhoun, Fred, 69–70
Carrying a Concealed Weapon (CCW) permits, 39–40
cease-and-desist letters, 34–35, 41–45
cell phones
    emergency calls on, 75
    patron use of, 40
    See also phones
child abuse responders, 128–129
Child Protective Services (CPS), 129
children
    abandonment/neglect of, 37–38, 65–66
    abuse and, 128–129
    fighting, 80
    small, 64–65
citizen's arrests, 76, 78
clothing, 37
code words, 73–74
codes of conduct
    consistency and, 13
    posting and enforcing, 26–27
    review of, 110
    violators of, 54
    See also rules
comfort animals, 38–39, 57–58
common sense, 25–26
communication tools, 89–92
community partners, 121–131
condescension, 24, 89
consequence-based thinking, 94

consequences, 14, 20

consistency, 10, 13

contraband items, 39–40

cooperation

    levels of, 10–11

    promoting, 90–91

county mental health (CMH) hospital, 124–126

courageous management, 95

coworkers

    fear and, 9–10

    See also employees/staff

Crucial Conversations (Patterson, Grenny, McMillan, and Switzler), 48

customer service

    approaches for, 21–22

    code of quality, 24–26

    high-risk, training for, 94

    over the phone, 22–23

    sins of, 23–24

D

de Becker, Gavin, 9, 15–16, 44, 77

dependent adults, 66, 129–130

diet, 156

documentation, 19, 80

dogs, 38–39

domestic violence, 60–61, 130

drills, 113, 145

drinking, 40

drug sellers, 53–54

E

eating, 40

Ekman, Paul, 92–93

elder abuse responders, 129–130

elderly patrons, 66

emergency plans, 110–111, 113, 145. *See also* 911

empathy, 86–88

Employee Assistance Programs (EAP), 67–68

employees

    security culture and, 93–94

    security surveys of, 100–107

employees-only areas, 35

employees/staff

    assistance for, 67–68

    fearful, 9–10

    on library environment, 4–5

    on patron behavior, 6–7

equipment

    misuse of, 40–41

    theft of, 37

evacuation drills/plans, 95, 111

Exceptional Case Study Project, 42, 69

exercise, 155–156

F

Facial Action Coding System (FACS), 92

facial expressions, 92–93

facility security review, 141–142. *See also* site security surveys

fear-creating acts, 69–71

fiduciary instrument controls, 111–112, 143–144

fight-or-flight mode, 18

fire department, 112, 144

fire drills, 113

firearms, 39–40. *See also* shooters

first impressions, 25

first-aid procedures, 111, 143

friendliness, 25

Friesen, Wallace, 92

G

gang members, 51–52

Giffords, Gabrielle, 139

Gift of Fear, The (de Becker), 9, 44

Gladwell, Malcolm, 92

greetings, 24–25

Grenny, Joseph, 48

guns, 39–40. *See also* shooters

H

Herrera, Luis, 2

high-risk customer service training, 94

homeless advocacy groups, 121–123

homeless people, 2, 55–56
HR manuals, 110
Hunters and Howlers, 69–73, 94
hygiene issues, 57

I
information security, 111, 142
information technology policy, 40–41
Internet issues, 58–59
intimidation, 33
intuition, 9, 137

J
Jenkins, Debra, 71
Jenkins, Jerry, 86–87

K
Keen, Judy, 2

L
language issues, 63
last impressions, 26
law enforcement. *See* police
LEAPS model, 86–89
legal advice, for patrons, 66–67
liability issues, 78, 99–100, 101, 108
library environment
    changes in, 1–2, 6–7
    staffer comments on, 4–5
limits and boundaries
    importance of, 10
    over the phone, 23
listening skills, 86–88
Loughner, Jared Lee, 139

M
Mack, Robert, 19, 72
Marx, Patricia, 57–58
McMillan, Ron, 48
Megan's Law, 59–60
mental health services, 123–127
mentally ill patrons, 52
micro expressions, 92–93
Millan, Cesar, 39

misdemeanors, 76
multitasking, 25

N
911, 75–76, 111, 112, 117. *See also*
    emergency plans
Nordstrom, 133–134

O
Occupational Safety and Health
    Administration (OSHA), 84–85

P
panhandling, 31–32
paraphrasing, 88
parents, entitled, 62–63
Pareto principle, 120
patron behavior
    changes in, 3
    cooperativeness level and, 10–11
    rationalizations about, 11–12
    "reasonable" test and, 10
    reasons for, 5
    staffer comments on, 6–7
    when to intercede in, 8–10
patrons
    angry, 49, 89–92
    complaints from, 9
    dependent adults, 66
    disabled, 66
    domestic violence and, 60–61
    eccentric, 50–51
    elderly, 66
    entitled, 50
    entitled parents, 62–63
    gang members, 51–52
    homeless people, 55–56
    hygiene issues and, 57
    Internet issues and, 58–59
    mentally ill, 52
    needy, 50–51
    non-English speakers, 63
    Rules of Engagement with, 47–48
    sex offenders, 59–60

patrons (*cont.*)
    sexual behavior and, 62
    small children, 64–65
    stalkers, 61
    substance abusers, 53–54
    tax or legal advice and, 66–67
    threatening, 49–50
    training exercises regarding, 149–153
    unruly teenagers, 64
    vandals, 51. *See also* vandalism
Patterson, Kerry, 48
pedophiles, 59–60
perimeter security, 110, 141
personal hygiene, 57
personal self-defense, 79–81
personal space, 16, 47, 137
phones
    cell phones, 40, 75
    customer service over, 22–23
    patron use of, 40
Pinsky, Drew, 123
police
    calling, 73–76
    interaction checklist for, 144
    interactions with, 112
    mentally ill patrons and, 124–126
    perception of, 116
    working with, 117–120
policy and procedure review, 110–113, 142
pornography, 58–59
positive language, 27
preattack behaviors, 69–71
problem-oriented policing, 120
profiles, 14
prohibited items, 39–40
proxemic barriers, 16–17, 47, 138
psychological self-defense, 16

R
rationalizations, 11–12, 20
reading dangerous faces, 92–93
relaxation, 155
respect, 14
restraining orders, 34–35, 60–61, 112–113

restricted areas, 35
restrooms, misuse of, 37
Roosevelt, Teddy, 116
rules
    bending, 26
    patrons not following, 33
    violators of, 54
    See also codes of conduct
Rules of Engagement, 47–48
Run. Hide. Fight., 95–98
*Run. Hide. Fight. Surviving an Active
    Shooter Event*, 96, 98, 112

S
safe rooms, 95
safety and security
    themes, 13–15
    tips, 20
Secret Service Hands, 81
security
    approach to, 107–108
    culture of, 93–94
    improvements in, 93, 99–100
    top ten tips for, 137–138
security guards, 76–79, 112, 144
self-defense, 79–81
self-protection, 16–17
Sensitive Compartmented Information
    Facilities (SCIFs), 108–109
*Service America! Doing Business in the
    New Economy* (Albrecht), 23
service animals, 38–39, 57–58
sex offenders, 59–60
sexual behavior, 35, 62
shelter in place, 95
SHOCADID, 53
shoes, 37
shooters, 95–98, 112–113. *See also*
    firearms
site security surveys
    checklists for, 141–146
    conducting, 107–113
    employee survey for, 100–107
    follow-up for, 113–114, 146

implementation and, 113, 145
overview of, 99–100
policy review and, 110–113
process for, 110
report from, 113–114, 145
suggestions based on, 147–148
team for, 109
skates and skateboards, 36
sleep, stress management and, 156–157
sleeping, in library, 39
smoking, 31
soliciting, 31–32
staff. *See* employees/staff
staff development, 133–140
stalking, 60–61
stress management, 17–18, 155–157
stressful breathing, 17–18, 155
substance abusers, 53–54
summarizing, 89
suspicious activities, 85–86
Switzler, Al, 48

T
tax advice, for patrons, 66–67
teenagers
    fighting, 80
    unruly, 64
temporary restraining orders (TROs),
        34–35, 60–61, 112–113
theft, 36–37, 55, 143
Thompson, George, 86–89
thought stopping, 91–92
*Threat Assessment and Management
        Strategies* (Calhoun and Weston), 70
Threat Assessment Teams (TAT),
        94–95, 117
threats
    assessing and managing, 71–73

calling police for, 73–76
cease-and-desist letters and, 41–45
from patrons, 49–50
procedures for, 32–33
reading dangerous faces, 92–93
understanding, 69–71
Ticking Bombs (Albrecht), 19, 72
training, 94, 134–136, 149–153
trespassing, 35

U
USA Today, 2

V
vandalism, 36–37, 51, 76
vendor procedures, 111, 143
Verbal Judo Institute, 87
Verbal Judo: The Gentle Art of Persuasion
        (Thompson), 86–89
Veterans Affairs, 117
voice level, 47–48

W
weapons. *See* firearms; shooters
Weston, Steve, 69–70
working smart, 18–19
workplace violence
    definition of, 84
    overview of, 83
    perpetrators of, 84–85
    response plans for, 111, 112–113,
        144–145
    suspicious activities before, 85–86
    tools for prevention of, 93–95

Y
Young Frankenstein, 91